To Shelly –
Rest.
Julie Barnhu –

EXQUISITE: keenly felt
Matchless
consummate,
ethereal,
precise.
Profound
extensive,
wise,
intimate.

HOPE: desire and expectation rolled into One
Reward
confidence,
prize,
refuge.
Harbor
rest,
promise,
sanctuary.

Who doesn't need a dose of hope? And in a package we "get"? *Exquisite Hope*, by Julie Ann Barnhill. Ah . . . just what we need.

Elisa Morgan, President and CEO,
MOPS International

Julie Barnhill's done it again in *Exquisite Hope!* She's the girlfriend who makes me laugh out loud as she candidly reveals her foibles and insecurities. But better still, she's that trusted voice reminding me once again that God cares about my dreams—and *yours!*

Jane Johnson Struck, Editor,
TODAY'S CHRISTIAN WOMAN magazine

What Real Women Say
about Julie Ann Barnhill, her books, and her workshops. . . .

There wasn't a page in this book that didn't have "ME" written all over it.

Thank you for writing such a hilarious, yet frank book about the wonder of God's AMAZING grace. You've exposed your life and experiences so that others may see how scandalous God's grace is! I can't wait to read *Radical Forgiveness*—I really need it!

I am a "new" Christian. I've often felt overwhelmed with the daunting task of *becoming* a Christian mom, wife, friend, employee. . . . Your simple and laugh-out-loud instruction has given me hope.

I love *Radical Forgiveness*! What more can I say? I laughed as hard as if you were sitting with me! This book is full of what I need to hear! You go, girl. One big hanky wave for this fabulous book!

Even though I was raised in the church, I've made some very bad choices. It's a good thing God's grace is in never-ending supply, 'cuz I sure have used quite a bit of it! Thank you for showing me how to give those things to the cross and allow scandalous grace to take care of the rest!

For the first time in 53 years I'm admitting my scorched places. I had them all along and just didn't recognize them . . . or how they were affecting my life and relationships. Thanks a bunch—from the bottom of my heart!

I cried when I read *Radical Forgiveness* because you have made the concept of forgiveness so *personal*. It touched my heart in such a way that I can only humbly say thank you, and then thank God for forgiveness and salvation. Otherwise I would be surely lost with no place to go but down.

Three years ago, when I was 37, I found out my dad was not my biological father. My mom was raped by someone she knew. When you talked about the boy and the *A* on his forehead, and how he is the reminder of sin, that is how I have felt—only I have an *R* for product of Rape . . . and a reminder of a painful time for my mother. I know that God turns ugly situations into beautiful blessings, but some days I require more grace than others. I will continue to pray about it, but in the meantime your message reinforced to me that God is the only Father I truly need.

I have been in therapy for 13 years because of my scorched places. I came to hear you with a broken heart, but left with hope.

Thank you for being candid. I'm 23 and getting married in September. I don't even like to read, but God put this book in my hand for a reason—because I needed to learn how to accept myself. I'll probably have the same acne as I do now for the rest of my life, but now I realize that's not even important.

Radical Forgiveness came into my life at such a perfect time. A member of my church had just told another church member something that I had shared with her in confidence. I have a lot to forgive. *Radical* gave me a place to start.

I've always been insecure, and lately I've gained a lot of weight. This makes me feel even worse about myself. Thank you for showing me how to stop comparing myself to others.

I have never felt like I was what God wanted—like I was a very good Christian. When you said God accepts us even with our mistakes and faults, a warm feeling of peace came over me. I wanted to run up and give you a great big hug!

Until *Scandalous Grace,* I really never believed that other women thought the things that I did. I thought I was the only one who weighed herself every day.

I am a single mother of two wonderful girls, ages 11 and 7 And yet it is like you have lived my life in parts . . . as if I were writing the book myself! It is so wonderful to know that I am "normal."

You are hilarious, yet you touch the secret places of my mind and my heart. You have made my entire life better!

You've given me permission to accept myself, while not making excuses for attitudes and behaviors that are destructive.

I attended one of your break-out sessions at a Hearts at Home conference because I thought it would make me laugh. And I did (as did everyone in the room) because I really related to your candor and your story. But I also walked away with a lot more—God's *Scandalous Grace,* his *Radical Forgiveness,* and also new hope. I can't wait until *Exquisite Hope* is available. These are books all of us "girls" need to read!

I've been a "mess" more times than I care to remember. Some-times that makes it hard to believe God still loves me. But instead of rolling my eyes at another "God loves you" book, you had me hooked from the first page.

I can't tell you how liberating it is to find out that there are so many other women out there just like me. Only the addresses change! More liberating still is to know that God's grace and his radical forgiveness are sufficient.

I've read lots of self-help books, but none of them impacted my life like your workshop.

You have *got* to get your own talk show. I have never laughed so hard in my life!

Talk about a timely, appropriate message for me and my friends. You just keep on doin' what you're doin', girlfriend!

OTHER BOOKS BY JULIE ANN BARNHILL

Radical Forgiveness

Scandalous Grace

She's Gonna Blow! Real Help for Moms Dealing with Anger

'Til Debt Do Us Part

Exquisite Hope

*The something more
you've been longing for!*

JULIE ANN BARNHILL

TYNDALE HOUSE PUBLISHERS, INC.
WHEATON, ILLINOIS

Visit Tyndale's exciting Web site at www.tyndale.com

TYNDALE is a registered trademark of Tyndale House Publishers, Inc.

Tyndale's quill logo is a trademark of Tyndale House Publishers, Inc.

Exquisite Hope

Designed by Luke Daab

Edited by Ramona Cramer Tucker

Published in association with the literary agency of Alive Communications, Inc., 7680 Goddard Street, Suite 200, Colorado Springs, CO 80920.

Unless otherwise noted, Scripture quotations are taken from *THE MESSAGE*. Copyright © 1993, 1994, 1995, 1996, 2000, 2001, 2002. Used by permission of NavPress Publishing Group.

Scripture quotations marked NASB are taken from the *New American Standard Bible,* © 1960, 1962, 1963, 1968, 1971, 1972, 1973, 1975, 1977 by The Lockman Foundation. Used by permission.

Scripture quotations marked NIV are taken from the *Holy Bible,* New International Version®. NIV®. Copyright © 1973, 1978, 1984 by International Bible Society. Used by permission of Zondervan Publishing House. All rights reserved.

Scripture quotations marked "NKJV" are taken from the New King James Version. Copyright © 1979, 1980, 1982 by Thomas Nelson, Inc. Used by permission. All rights reserved.

Library of Congress Cataloging-in-Publication Data

Barnhill, Julie Ann, date.
    Exquisite hope : the something more you've been longing for / Julie Ann Barnhill.
      p. cm.
    Includes bibliographical references.
    ISBN-13: 978-1-4143-0032-0 (sc)
    ISBN-10: 1-4143-0032-8 (sc)
    1. Hope—Religious aspects—Christianity.   2. Christian life.   I. Title.
    BV4638.B36 2005
    234'.25—dc22   2005006495

Printed in the United States of America

11   10   09   08   07   06   05
7   6   5   4   3   2   1

To The One
who is ever Faithful,
ever True

Contents

Acknowledgments

$\mathcal{F}$unny, but the circle of people who choose to hang around me during my writing spells seems to be dwindling every year. It must be a reflection of my dynamic personality during those times!

I think I filled four pages of acknowledgments in my first book. While this fifth time around will be shorter, it certainly won't be any less sweet or sincere in its message of thanks.

So here goes

Ramona Cramer Tucker: Once again you have challenged me to search for the best word, rather than the easiest; to stick with completing a sane, transitional statement rather than chucking it and calling it quits. You have polished my rough and dented draft into another book I am proud to have worked with you on.

Karen Watson and Carol Traver: For believing (and acquiring) my thoughts on grace, forgiveness, and hope. You've spoiled me with your kindness, business savvy, and unflagging confidence in what can be done through humor and honesty.

Rick, Kristen, Ricky Neal, and Patrick: Thanks for saying yes when I asked yet one more time, "Do you mind if I read this to you?" and for consistently delivering excellent fodder for stories and illustrations. You know this already, but let me say it again: I love you forever.

Gracie Malone: You seem to "know" just when to call, my friend. Thanks for hammering out those stubborn chapters and helping me "hear" my thoughts again.

Hope deferred makes the heart sick,
But desire fulfilled is a tree of life.
Proverbs 13:12, NASB

This is the journey of exquisite yearning, exquisite promise,
exquisite and eternal belonging . . .

Ɔ Know a Place

Ɔ'm *baaack,* girls!

And, may I add, I'm tired.

If you could see me right now *(and let's all just stop and give thanks that Mr. Microsoft hasn't patented* that *algorithm yet),* clothing attire alone would bear expert witness. Yes, indeedy, nothing quite says, "Depleted, spent, and exhausted" like a pair of ratty, plaid, flannel lounge pants, a red Mickey Mouse fleece pullover speckled with fabric pilling, and puffy, neon green, Steve Madden house slippers roughly the size of Rhode Island.

Ah, yes, the "What to Wear" wardrobe of choice for overtaxed women everywhere. . . .

But my style of dress *(or lack thereof)* isn't the lone indicator of diminishing energy reserves. No, soon after completing *Radical Forgiveness,* I somehow managed to misplace my brain. As a result, I've been unable to retain conversational nouns *("Would you please hand me that, um, thing right over by the, uh, place that I sit down when I come in the, er, oh, just forget it!")* in the hollow confines of what I once endearingly referred to as "My Mind." The loss was exacerbated, no doubt, by a crammed social calendar of parent-teacher conferences and visits to the dermatologist for adult onset acne.

So now there are approximately 32 Post-it notes precipitously dangling and vying for attention around the dusty frame of my Dell flat-screen, um, box-looking gizmo. Scribbled on said Post-its are passwords for Web sites long forgotten, bank balances for both business and family checking accounts *(with exclamation points noting less-than-positive numbers),* as well as random sparks of inspirational genius hastily recorded for possible chapter development *(none of which I am currently able to read or decipher, mind you).* There is even order information for Hype Energy Drink, which claims to be full of vitamins, guarana, and natural fruit juices to give you a great-tasting energy drink that refreshes and reenergizes. *(Hmm, wonder if I can order that in IV drip form?)*

All around my computer, on every surface of space that can be filled in my office, in the tape-recorded messages left on my answering machine, as well as the not-to-be-forgotten minor details of marriage, motherhood, and friendship, there are reminders of what I need to do—reminders of who I am to be.

And it makes me tired.

I think you know exactly what I'm talking about. Either that, or you're lying.

Call me crazy, but there's a reason many of you chose to journey with me through the stories and confessions of *Scandalous Grace* and *Radical Forgiveness.* We've laughed so hard we've snorted *(and sundry* other *physical responses, but I won't go there)* as author to reader, friend to friend, while peeling back and sandblasting the pointless veneer of pretending we have it all together. *(And may I just say I have enjoyed every minute of it?)*

Many of us have not only embraced our cellulite but, more importantly in the grand scheme of life, embraced the reality of being a mess of magnificent proportions. And for those who haven't? Well, they've extended scads of lavish grace toward us who have. We've joined in and "let it go"—all the while waving a girlfriend hanky of agreement for any number of XX chromosome issues and foibles.

So, in honor of our time spent together in previous outings— as well as an official, "I'm so glad you're reading one of my books for the first time!" welcome from me if you haven't joined us before—here goes. As your friendly, messy, "I Lost My Mind" author and all-around companion, I'd like to provide a final offering of girlfriend hanky-waving truth. You know the drill— grab a hanky or another wave-friendly item of choice, stand up, and . . . *(well, in light of my condition, let's just sit down for this round, shall we?)* sit down. Prepare to agree, disagree, or simply find an excuse to be free from that tired old underwire bra you're currently wearing.

Ready? Okay, here we go. . . .

✳ If you've ever attended (as an adult) a concert of your favorite band when you were in high school (i.e., Journey), then looked around in alarm and asked your husband or friend, "We don't look as old as everyone else here, do we?" give me a geriatric hanky wave. *(Careful—don't hurt yourself, girlfriend!)*

✳ If you feel the same way I do about getting your breasts slammed annually by cold bookends, all in the guise of a mammogram, give me an *uh, ouch* hanky wave.

✳ If you've ever gotten a call from your doctor requesting you
to schedule another bookend moment because your films
were somehow misplaced, give me an outraged hanky wave.

✳ If your neighbor just dropped off a whole plate of brownies
and you had not one, but *four* of them in the first 10
seconds, give me a hanky wave.

✳ If you have ever prayed that the car in front of you would
get the speeding ticket, not you, give me a hanky wave.

✳ If you have ever told God, "God, if you'll just do this one
thing for me, then I'll never do that one thing again," give
me a hanky wave.

✳ If you have ever been tempted to smash your alarm clock
into oblivion, give me a hanky wave.

✳ If your cat or dog or fish or child has ever received the brunt
of your bad day, give me a hanky wave.

✳ If you've ever listened to yourself talking and at the same
time thought, *Shut up! Just shut up!* give me a silent hanky
wave.

✳ If you long for "Calgon, take me away!" and you haven't
even gotten out of bed yet, give me a hanky wave.

✳ If you know heaven is out there, but it just seems too far
away to matter much on an average day, give me a hanky
wave.

How well I relate! Each and every hanky wave brings to mind
the "to do" and "to be" realities of my life:

the invoices I need to pay
the phone calls I need to follow up

the packages I need to mail

the e-mails I need to write

the lessons I need to prepare

the research material I need to gather

the Bible questions I should be able to answer

the broken, wounded women I should be able to encourage

the appointments I need to keep

the relationships I need to mend

the exercise I should begin *(groan)*

etc.

etc.

etc., already!

(Heavy exhale of breath)

Each and every "to be" and "to do" adds up—one on top of the other, piggybacking and hopscotching from one monstrous pile to the other—until finally, fingers flying across cyberwaves, I surf an Expedia.com SOS, desperate to find an oasis, longing to find a slow *(and cheap)* cruise to paradise.

✳ ✳ ✳

Paradise—hmm. Now there's a concept a girl could shake a hanky at.

In January 2004 I embarked on my first Caribbean cruise with my then 15-year-old daughter, Kristen. She and I are cut from the same cloth when it comes to climate preferences, so anytime the mercury drops below 69.9 degrees Fahrenheit, we're pretty much miserable. And since we live in the state of Illinois during winter months, well, we're miserable a good six to seven months out of the year. Not that anyone else would even notice. Oh, no. Far be it from either of us to whine, mope, grumble, bellyache, snivel, grouse, gasp, or murmur about cold-weather conditions or the place in which we live.

Nope, not us.

All right, for the sake of the story *(and truth in writing),* let's just say we find Illinois to be the most miserable place on the face of the planet during the months of November through May—late May—and the prospect of sailing to tropical ports of the Western Caribbean to be, well, heavenly.

So that January afternoon we left behind wind-chill factors, icy mixes of snow, and those brittle gusts of wind that suck the life *(and humor)* straight out of you. And onward we flew to Orlando, boarding a Carnival Cruise ship at Cape Canaveral. A mere 10 hours later we arrived on the sunny shores of blissful Pirate Island.

For five days and four nights, I basked in the rays of sunshine. I swung for hours in a hammock on Blue Lagoon Island, thinking how absolutely perfect the world would be without snow.

There were no e-mails to answer.

No cell phones to take or avoid.

No chapters to write.

No deadlines to meet.

No conferences to attend.

All I had to do was rest . . . and all I had to be was me.

Paradise, indeed.

But here's the best part, girls. I unearthed My Mind on those heavenly shores of the Caribbean *(who'd a thunk it?)*. Yes, it was discovered deep beneath bone-warming rays of sunshine and comforting tides of ocean waves. As a result, I found both My Mind and my physical body believing in the restorative power of hope.

Hope?

Yes, hope.

You see, time and time again, I have found myself right where I was at the beginning of that vacation as well as where I am today.

Restless.

A tad bit irritable.

And more than a tad bit apprehensive and desperate for a reminder of past felt peace, a sense of belonging, and the hope of things eternal.

Yes, I'm the one who told you to look at everything through the following question: In the light of eternity, does this matter? Author, heal thyself!

Yet time after time I find myself flailing about, having lost my moorings to the anchor tethering my life. Quite honestly, there is an overall sense of predictability about such things, and I think I know why—at least in part. I'm quickly approaching the 4-0 marker of life and, as such, have had ample time to study my habits *(good and bad)*, multiple quirks, and also the deficits of my personality and character. I've come to understand certain inevitabilities that will influence factors both in faith and life.

No matter your age, perhaps you will relate—as a woman eager to dissect the predictable reruns of her life.

INEVITABLE RERUN #1: I WILL RUN MYSELF RAGGED.

Take it to the bank, baby—of this you can be sure. It doesn't matter how many books I may read regarding balance in life, work, and love (*my last attempt was during the summer of 1991*), or how many times I come to the end of my rope and drop like a sack of lead, or how many times I've looked at my calendar and realized I've committed myself to three different events at the same time, it always, always, always happens.

It all goes back to my "all or nothing" personality. I promise the moon, with full intention of delivering but resemble a madwoman during the process. I love deeply, grieve profoundly, and dream humongous dreams of what can be, thereby expending much emotion, angst, and "why not?" imaginings. But that means I have little, if anything, left over for what remains—huh, a little thing called "Real Life." You know, the one that comes with accessories such as a husband, children, work deadlines, and pants I can no longer fit into.

But do I admit this? Do I restructure my reading, my rope, or my calendar to make room for less ragged and more rest? (*Do you?*) Of course *I* don't. I just keep at it—plugging away and throwing back one Red Bull after the other because there really is little margin for ragged in my world.

INEVITABLE RERUN #2: I WILL LOSE SIGHT OF WHAT IS IMPORTANT.

Many of you reading this book may have been raised with a church background similar to mine. I attended Sunday morning church services as early as I can remember (age four) and participated in Vacation Bible School programs and a program called Girls in Action, where young girls could learn more about foreign missions work and the Bible, throughout elementary school. It was a given, once summer rolled around, that I would either attend or work as a counselor at one or two church camp programs.

Overall, I always found it enjoyable learning about God. I never wrestled much with the concept of a Creator—a God who lives in a place called Heaven. Nor did I find it difficult to believe in Jesus as God's Son. In fact, I really loved that idea. I'll never forget reading for the first time a story found in the New Testament book of Mark:

"While he was still talking, some people came from the leader's house and told him, 'Your daughter is dead. Why bother the Teacher any more?'

Jesus overheard what they were talking about and said to the leader, 'Don't listen to them; just trust me.'

He permitted no one to go in with him except Peter, James, and John. They entered the leader's house and pushed their way through the gossips looking for a story and neighbors bringing in casseroles. Jesus was abrupt: 'Why all this busybody grief and gossip? This child isn't dead; she's sleeping.' Provoked to sarcasm, they told him he didn't know what he was talking about.

But when he had sent them all out, he took the child's father and mother, along with his companions, and entered the child's room. He clasped the girl's hand and said, '*Talitha koum*,' which means, 'Little girl, get up.' At that, she was up and walking around! This girl was twelve years of age. They, of course, were all beside themselves with joy."[1]

Now really, who couldn't love a Jesus like that? He was kind and cared a lot about children.[2] And he even brought a little girl back to life! How cool is that? And so I did choose to love him with a head-over-heels, all my heart, soul, strength, and mind kind of commitment. I suppose that's why this particular rerun of life eats away at me so much.

I know, thanks to great teaching during those multiple trips to church, that the life I live is God's alone. I know each breath comes from him. I know he's numbered the hairs on my head *(and forearms)*. So if I know these things, why do I do the things I do or lose sight of those things that are most important? Am I simply a shallow, self-centered Christian pinhead who doesn't recognize such things in her life? *(Send comments to: julie@juliebarnhill.com.)*

If I'm really being honest, *I've lost hope that I truly believed the Bible verse I memorized as a young teenager and have quoted year after year since: "In Him we live and move and have our being."*[3] Next time you see a puppy chasing its tail, think of me and this rerun. For that's how I see myself: *knowing* it's all about Jesus logically and concretely, yet still managing to lose sight of what's important, over and over, around and around, again.

INEVITABLE RERUN #3: I'LL LOSE HOLD OF LIFE'S ANCHOR—HOPE.

Do you see a pattern in these three reruns?

First I overextend myself, wear out, and grow weary. This leaves me with a tendency to lose sight of what's important, thereby rendering me weak. And then I lose my grasp of The One who gives me life and makes my life meaningful.

And when these three things occur? Well, it's all over except for the Prozac.

Be it momentary or a long-fought struggle through weeks, months, or even years, losing hope always hits like a sucker punch to the gut. It goes against my nature—this loss of confident expectation, and it never, ever feels right or pleasing.

And so hope finds me (us) oftentimes stranded between dreaming and wishing.

Between faith and despair.

Between the way things are and the way we wish them to be.

Oh, yes. I'm old enough now to know there are thousands of women who suffer from soul sickness as a result of shattered dreams. Dreams built on hope—hope for restored relationships, upward-moving career developments, an anticipated marriage, healing for the one that fell apart at the seams and ripped our heart to shreds. And hope for doing better, or being different, or anything *other* than what we've actually accomplished.

Or am I getting the cart before the horse?

✳   ✳   ✳

What, exactly, is hope?

Is it simply wishing really, really, *really* hard?

Is it the power of positive thinking—something we slap on over fear or apathy as we pull our spiritual bootstraps higher and higher in a pseudo-spiritual *I think I can, I think I can* little-red-engine confession of faith?

Is hope real?

Can you touch it? See it? Smell it or plant it and harvest more of said commodity?

I don't recall ever officially applying for hope. What about you? So how is it we feel it deep within our soul and grieve in an even deeper place when we feel as though it's lost or has been taken from us?

And what purpose does hope serve in my life . . . in yours?

Is hope just another *good* feeling we get when things go well?

A crutch of convenience we lean on when things go—well—horrible, and we find ourselves unable to understand or explain why?

(And what's with this compulsive need/pressure to explain everything, anyway? Maybe that's a book one of you could write!)

Why do we need hope?

And while we're asking *(okay—I'm asking, you're pondering),* is it possible to separate the virtuous trio of faith, hope, and love?[4] Can you have one without the others?

Does one "possess" hope, or are you "given" it? And perhaps just as importantly, has Wal-Mart found a way to slap a smiley face on it and sell it?

Where and with whom does hope begin?

And where does it ultimately lead . . . or *end?*

Some questions, huh?

I'm guessing you are far more like me than you may care to believe. That's why I know many of you have dared to dream and hope somewhere along the way of life and have come up empty-handed—empty-hearted. I know you most likely ache to believe dreams matter. Better said, you ache to believe *your* dreams matter—to know that those dreams are endorsed and sponsored by The One who authors all such things.[5]

Despite age differences, socioeconomic status, ethnic backgrounds, or any number of extenuating circumstances, we all bear an indelible mark of connection as women. How can I know this? Because I've read and responded to your e-mails, spoken one-on-one with you after conference events, stayed up until 3:00 AM talking and laughing in front of a crackling fireplace while eating decadent Texas sheet cake, and returned phone messages after meeting you via the Internet, magazine articles, radio interviews, or television appearances airing in places as far away as Budapest, Hungary; Stephenage, England; Singapore, Asia; and as near as Bushnell, Illinois; Opelika, Alabama; and Duluth, Minnesota.

I believe there is a place where tired women like me (and you) can find reprieve from life's inevitabilities. I believe there is a place of *safe harbor* from our frenetic living, *sanctuary* for our hesitant faith, and *confident expectation* for what lies ahead both today and a hundred years from now.

I believe in a place called Hope.

Hope demonstrated through dreams and longings.

Hope as the ultimate destination package.

Hope as a noun, found in the person of Jesus Christ.

Forget about dog-paddling or bobbing along through life like an untethered cork, girls! In this, our third literary outing, we'll bask in the undulating nearness of hope. This is all about living and believing and trusting in The One who is able to keep us secure in his grip. This is all about anchoring our past, present, and future to tranquil and profound hope.

Many of us *(how I hope* all *of us)* have had the canvas of our life marked by the distinguishable color palate of the Divine. His strokes of chartreuse grace have inundated our lives and quenched scorched places. Swaths of magenta forgiveness have rescued and redeemed us from our secrets and sin, leading us to this final, turquoise-hued moment. Now hope beckons us to lift our heads a bit higher—encourages us to gaze toward life's horizon with a bit more confidence. And it urges us to come away and find rest.

Rest?

Yes, lasting rest.

So what do you think? Are you ready for a relaxing read and a bit of refreshment for your heart, mind, and soul? Are you ready to consider a few of the questions I proposed a few paragraphs back? And are you willing to believe, even slightly, in The One who embodies all hope, who knows each and every one of our dreams, and even now is preparing a place of eternal sanctuary for each and every one who will trust him?[6]

Then let's go!

I've found a perfect spot to settle down. It's right on the beach *(my favorite place in the entire world),* and we can set up our lounge chairs to catch the best rays.

Here—take some of this sunscreen if you're prone to burning.

Ah, let's burrow our toes and feet about ankle deep into the damp, cool sand. That palm tree provides the right amount of shade, don't you think?

Hmm. Everything is just about perfect, except we're missing a carbonated beverage with a slice of lime and one of those colorful little paper umbrellas. *(Forgoing a Pepsi addiction, I order 7-Up. "Uh, waiter!")*

As we wait for Coco the cabana boy to return, in your mind's eye, listen closely to the sounds. . . .

Pebbles tumbling in the surf . . .

Oystercatchers calling as they feed among the rocks . . .

Seagulls and surfside songbirds contributing to the song of the sea . . .

The rhythm of the waves lapping lazily against the shore . . .

Oh, my! Now *this* is just what the author ordered. Are you comfy? Shall we continue on, or is a Caribbean siesta in order? Okay, onward then to Chapter 2, as the magnificent mysteries of hope are revealed.

Exquisitely Yours,
Julie Ann Barnhill

P.S. Pass me that box of Ho Hos, would ya?

I Love a Mystery

"Perhaps you can solve a mystery."

Those powerful words were spoken in the groundbreaking and highly popular television program dominating the television airwaves in 1988. My husband and I were newlyweds and we loved watching NBC's newest program. It wasn't a reality show, as we know them today, nor could it be considered a documentary. It was something altogether new and in between. Each week millions of viewers *(Rick and me included)* would sit by their television and wait as creepy theme music began to play and veteran screen actor Robert Stack appeared in what would soon become his trademark trench coat.

Mr. Stack's *Untouchables* fame was lost on our generation. But after watching or, more importantly, listening to one program narrated in his distinctive menacing baritone voice, we were fans—hook, line, and sinker. Intonating the gravity of each episode, Mr. Stack would either introduce a murder case, a missing person story, or a purported paranormal occurrence. Each tale would be reenacted and would offer as much information as possible to those tuning in to watch. More than once I nearly did myself in while making a wild dash back from a commercial break in hopes of hearing that distinctive voice challenge viewers across the country, "If you or someone you know has any information regarding the details of this program, contact our *Unsolved Mysteries* toll-free hotline."

I'm telling you, girls, all across America family members eyed family members, co-workers sized up co-workers, and neighbors suspiciously studied their next-door neighbors. Each and every one of us said to someone else at one time or another, "Hey, is it just me, or does Harold look just like that guy who's wanted on *Unsolved Mysteries*?" These unsolved true stories of crime and strange disappearances were tantalizing. And each of us longed to be the one who did indeed help "solve a mystery."

Okay, with such heavy thoughts, it's now time to take a break. I think I'll enjoy one of those Ho Hos, then dive into one of my favorite pastimes: enjoying a great whodunit-keep-me-on-my-toes-guessing mystery read. There is certainly a place for television programming such as *Unsolved Mysteries.* But for my money, nothing beats a well-crafted story kicking off with an "it was a dark and stormy night" setting. Give me lots and lots of foreboding thunderstorms and shadows. Follow it up with cleverly and mysteriously interspersed shady characters, heroes, red herrings, villains, and overlapping plot lines, joyously culminating in a satisfying "Aha!" wrap-up of revelation.

After all, I cut my first mystery teeth on the stories of *Encyclopedia Brown,* the perennial children's mystery series' favorite since time immemorial. Please tell me you remember Encyclopedia and his best friend, Sally! She was the female version of Watson to Encyclopedia's Sherlock. And there was, of course, their evil nemesis, Bugs Meany. Why, even the sound of his name sent shivers up and down my spine.

Each book was filled with stand-alone mystery chapters that offered inventive plots and more than a fair amount of cleverly thought-out clues. But the best part was that all the solutions to the mysteries were put in the *back* of the book. It was perfect for readers like me! You didn't have to know the solution to the mystery until you decided to look. Bookworms like me read those chapters time and time again until finally waving a flag of surrender and checking in with Encyclopedia's expert detective work.

After Encyclopedia I moved on, of course, to *Nancy Drew* and *The Hardy Boys*. I have to admit I was far more interested in Frank and Joe than I ever was in Nancy. I faithfully watched teen heartthrobs Shaun Cassidy and Parker Stevenson play Frank and Joe every other Sunday night on ABC television. Nancy, played by teen actress Pamela Sue Martin, just took valuable airtime away from those cute Hardy boys, in my opinion.

I would check the mysteries out from the library, read as many as I could in the days leading up to Sunday, then press my face to the television screen and see how true Hollywood translated the books to screen. *(It was to be the first of many disappointing experiences. Don't even get me started on* The Pelican Brief *or the novel* A Prayer for Owen Meany.*)*

And so my fascination grew. Book by book, author by author, until the Grand Dame of mystery writing took center stage with an earlier-released book, *Where Are the Children?* I don't think I ever slept through the night after that one *(mouth hanging open in hyperventilation mode)*! Mrs. Geraldine Stroemer had my name on the Brunswick Public Library waiting list for every one of Mary Higgins Clark's newest releases *(although my mom signed off on a couple due to questionable content. I didn't much like that)*. I then jumped onto the alphabet series of Sue Grafton and attempted to read the mind of James Patterson. Now that's a scary place. James liked his mystery mixed with a lot of body parts and mayhem, which failed to mix well with my weak and like-to-be-free-of-body-parts stomach.

With the exception of J. Patterson, I could lose myself for hours and hours reading those books. And no matter how carefully I tried to pay attention to cues and clues, no matter how I tried to get into the head of the main character or bad guy, no matter how I tried to change my thinking to another point of view, I could never solve the mystery.

Now, it's important to note the vast difference in said solving of mysteries. There were those which, when revealed, caused you to nod, smile a bit, and say to yourself, "Oh, yes. I see it now. Of course it was Miss Scarlet, in the study, with the hammer."

Nothing shocking, nothing earth-shattering.

But then there were *The Others*.

The Others were those books (and authors) you absolutely lived for. The ones you kept checking the library to see if they had arrived yet. The ones you begged your mom to buy the paperback copy for so you could have it all to yourself. Why? Because you knew—within the deepest, most "I love a mystery" part of your literary soul—that you would get to the last chapter, perhaps, or even the last six or seven pages, and be completely blown away by the who, what, when, and why of the resolution. And it goes without saying *(almost)* that you didn't so much respond to *The Others* as react in high velocity, jumping up and down screaming ALL CAPS of amazement, "I NEVER thought it would be HER! I NEVER would have guessed that in a MILLION years!"

A great mystery revealed isn't unlike getting hit by a Mac truck, all the while thinking, *Let me do that again!*

Well, I've got another mystery for you to think about—to investigate, so to speak. It's full of intrigue as it reveals the heart of God toward women like you and me. But first things first. Let's start with this clue *(i.e., overarching statement of truth)*: Christianity is a baffling mystery to many people.

I doubt I'm the only woman of faith who has attempted to explain some foundational truth about Jesus, about the three-in-one God, or some thoroughly Christian principle *(such as "love those who do not love you"),* only to be greeted with a dazed pair of eyes. I'm sure I'm not the only one who has had someone they know and love say, "I just don't get this Jesus thing you have going in your life." And I know I'm not the only one who has felt guilty, wondering why it is I can't seem to communicate the reality of who Jesus is and why he is important in my life *(especially those of us who call ourselves communicators).*

But I've come to realize it's not all about me and my inability to get through. The truth is: Christ indeed *is* a mystery. Forget what we do or say or attempt to explain. People looking at Christ alone—apart from his followers in all their sincere good-ness and foul-ups, apart from the organized church and its per-ceived list of dos and don'ts—find him to be an enigma . . . and his followers, quite frankly, to be a little bit crazy.

Respected theologian A. W. Tozer once wrote of this craziness in his work, *Roots of Righteousness:*

𝒜 real Christian is an odd number anyway. He feels supreme love for One whom he has never seen, talks familiarly every day to Someone he cannot see, expects to go to heaven on the virtue of Another, empties himself in order to be full, admits he is wrong so he can be declared right, goes down in order to get up, is strong when he is weakest, richest when he is poorest, and happiest when he feels worst. He dies so he can live, forsakes in order to have, gives away so he can keep, sees the invisible, hears the inaudible, and knows that which passeth knowledge.[1]

Those of us who believe personally in God and his Son, Jesus Christ, are a most peculiar lot, wouldn't you agree?[2] But this is truly what we believe. We believe in God—not a god but I Am,[3] God of Abraham, Isaac, and Jacob, the God of Israel.[4] We believe I Am spoke the earth into existence.[5] I'll not argue with you regarding whether it was a literal six days or if each one consisted of a thousand years.[6] Whatever the time period of creation, God was clearly in charge. But Christians pray and expect to hear *(how crazy is that?!)* from this God.[7] And we believe I Am sent his Son to rescue our life, redeem our heart, and engage in a lifelong, eternal relationship with us.[8]

Our good friend, the apostle Paul, once again is the bearer of great news. This man who passionately used to hate Christians was chosen, by God, to reveal the Mystery of the Ages. Let's see what he has to say.

"𝒯 his mystery has been kept in the dark for a long time, but now it's out in the open. God wanted everyone, not just Jews, to know this rich and glorious secret inside and out, regardless of their background, regardless of their religious standing. The mystery in a nutshell is just this: Christ is in you; therefore you can look forward to sharing in God's glory. It's that simple."[9]

I love the last part of these verses as found in another translation, "Christ in you, the hope of glory."[10]

Who-ha! In case you didn't notice, we just got hit by the Mac truck! Everything *(and I do mean everything)* we believe regarding life on this planet as well as our hope in the life to come, comes as a result of this magnificent mystery: Christ lives in each of us.

This seemingly simple fact never ceases to perplex and amaze me. I've often prayed that I would never get to a point in my life of faith where I ho-hummed such Eternal Mysteries. I've often made myself *(as well as my three children on occasion)* speak this truth aloud.

So let's do just that right now.

We spoke "Let It Go!" truth in *Scandalous Grace*.

We waved our hands dramatically as we spoke truth regarding our being "a mess of magnificent proportions" while experiencing *Radical Forgiveness*.

And so we come to a new truth in *Exquisite Hope*. The only thing I'm going to ask you to do, however, is to change the pronoun *you* to a proper noun—your name. Let me demonstrate: "Christ in Julie, the hope of glory."

Are you ready to give it a go? Okay, on the count of three: 1, 2, 3.

"Christ in _____, the hope of glory!"

May I just say that I'm getting goose bumps thinking about each and every one of you reading that mysterious truth with your name included? Wouldn't it be something if we could press a record button and tape each voice, each name, and then hear it in beautiful chorus? *(Or maybe you think I'm giving an excellent example of that crazy Christian stuff mentioned a few sentences back.)*

Do you realize how exquisite this hope is?

Do you grasp the magnitude of the fact that God *chose* to solve this mystery through the life, death, and resurrection of his only Son, Jesus, and then *chose* to reveal the mystery to Jew and Gentile alike *(as well as generation after generation to come)* through the apostle Paul? Did you know up until the time God chose to reveal this mystery through Paul that the angels themselves had longed to understand the mystery?[11]

The theological tentacles of this Mystery reach as far as his forgiveness.[12] And that is *infinitely far!*

While I can't even begin to wrap my brain around all the tentacles of the Mystery, these things I do know and understand: Jesus Christ is the sum of all things. "He set it all out before us in Christ, a long-range plan in which everything would be brought together and summed up in him, everything in deepest heaven, everything on planet earth. It's in Christ that we find out who we are and what we are living for."[13] Jesus is the eternal hope God had in mind.

"𝓛ong before we first heard of Christ and got our hopes up, he had his eye on us, had designs on us for glorious living, part of the overall purpose he is working out in everything and everyone."[14]

I love how Eugene Peterson paraphrases it:

"He was supreme in the beginning and—leading the resurrection parade—he is supreme in the end. From beginning to end he's there, towering far above everything, everyone. So spacious is he, so roomy, that everything of God finds its proper place in him without crowding. Not only that, but all the broken and dislocated pieces of the universe—people and things, animals and atoms—get properly fixed and fit together in vibrant harmonies, all because of his death, his blood that poured down from the Cross."[15]

In Christ we see all the riches,[16] all the blessings,[17] and all the wisdom[18] of God's glory.

Christ is the mystery of redemption revealed—the Good News made available to man and woman alike, to Jews and Gentiles, as well as rich and poor, educated and simple. And he dwells in our hearts![19] This is what separates Christianity *(and Jesus)* from any other religious creed. How marvelous it is to consider that God would *choose* to dwell in us! And as a result of his choosing to fill our lives with his presence, we possess the riches of his glory and his grace.

Ladies, more than anything, I desire to remind you of the anchoring hope of Jesus Christ. To remind you to make use of the hope and comfort found in the eternal steadfastness of God.

"In the same way God, desiring even more to show to the heirs of the promise the unchangeableness of His purpose, interposed with an oath, so that by two unchangeable things in which it is impossible for God to lie, we who have taken refuge would have strong encouragement to take hold of the hope set before us. This hope we have as an anchor of the soul, a hope both sure and steadfast."[20]

Isn't that just the way it feels at times? As though our very souls were ships being tossed up and down, to and fro, against the tidal waves of fear, apathy, doubt, and worry? Doesn't it seem at times as if our souls have lost anchor . . . as though they are at the discretionary whim of the next wave?

It need not be this way any longer.

Look again at the Bible verses you just read. I want to point out three specific anchors from them that you can use to tether your dreams, your eternal security, and your earthly hope.

ANCHOR #1: WE HAVE THE HOPE OF GOD'S UNCHANGING PURPOSE.

"Show to the heirs of the promise the unchangeableness of His purpose."

Okay, we're going to sail a bit deeper into the waters of girlfriend theology on this one. The unchangeableness of his purpose is found in the specific characteristics of the divine nature that make God *God,* in distinction from all that is finite *(i.e., you and me—all things created by God).* Singer and songwriter Steven Curtis Chapman summed this up quite well a few years ago with a song titled, "God Is God (and I Am Not)."

God, in the unchangeableness of his purpose, has no beginning or end *("I am the Alpha and the Omega"*[21]*).* We by creation are appointed a time to be born and a time to die *("appointed* *for men to die once"*[22]*).* God, in the unchangeableness of his purpose, is Omnipotent *(all-powerful),* Omniscient *(all-knowing),* and Omnipresent *(ever-present).* We, well, are not.

You're catching on, I'm sure. See—this is what makes this Mystery so extraordinary, ladies. I can't stop thinking of a quote I read some years ago:

O n the whole, I do not find Christians, outside of the catacombs, sufficiently sensible of conditions. Does anyone have the foggiest idea what sort of power we so blithely invoke? Or, as I suspect does no one believe a word of it? The churches are children playing on the floor with their chemistry sets, mixing up a batch of TNT to kill a Sunday morning. It is madness to wear ladies' straw hats to church; we should all be wearing crash helmets. Ushers should issue life preservers and signal flares; they should lash us to our pews. For the sleeping god may someday wake and take offense, or the waking god may draw us out to where we can never return.[23]

If I ever meet Ms. Dillard, I'm going to wrap my arms around her and give her a hearty girlfriend hug of appreciation. Has anyone ever said it any better? How bizarre that we, the first to hope in Christ Jesus,[24] should so quickly forget the majesty and power of The One we love. To paraphrase our friend the apostle Paul, "it just isn't right."

ANCHOR #2: WE HAVE THE HOPE AND PROMISE OF GOD'S UNCHANGING WORD.

"It is impossible for God to lie."

Pure and simple, God can't lie. It is impossible for him to

do so! And as such, that means any and all instructions he has given us regarding this life on earth and of the other still to be are true. You can count on every word. This is incredibly important to me. I've shared with you my own battles in the past with speaking truth and living out truth in the finer details of life, which no one but God himself most likely sees. I couldn't imagine believing in him, let alone trusting my eternal future to him, if this were not true.

Maybe you're thinking, *Yeah, Julie, but how would we know if God lied, anyway?* Good question. And I have a pretty easy answer for you. You'd know by understanding what he has promised in his revealed message to humankind—the Bible. I'm not going to recommend you read one more great book by one more great author *(although there are plenty who could fill a list).* I'm not going to recommend you listen to any radio pastors or television preachers. But I *am* going to challenge you to become a believing woman. A woman who knows what God has said about himself, about his plans for you, as well as his entire creation. A woman who believes the world that is to come after this one has been renovated and restored to its full glory. If you become a woman filled with the truth of God's promises, you'll find yourself clinging with even more abandon to The One who is Faithful and True.[25]

ANCHOR #3: WE HAVE THE HOPE OF HEAVEN.

"Laying hold of the hope set before us."

We'll discuss this at length in our final chapter, but for now, simply cast a thought toward the eternal expectation of a place filled with God and all his purposeful goodness. It isn't a fairy tale. It isn't a religious hoax. It isn't heaven on earth, right here, right now *(thank goodness)*. No, there is a place beyond belief— a place made without human hands—and a communal environment unlike anything ever attempted on earth.

When all of my study of things mysterious stirred more interest, I thought I'd dig a bit deeper and see what other mysteries God has revealed through Christ and to us. Here are a couple of interesting ones I found. I hope they spark in you a desire to read, study, and perhaps uncover a few of the incomparable truths of God for yourself.

In Matthew 13:11, we find Jesus speaking in parables. What's a parable, really? It's an imaginary story, yet its details actually could have happened. Its purpose is to illustrate or inculcate some higher spiritual truth.[26] Anyway, his disciples are asking him why. *(This resonates with me—I can all too easily picture my 10-year-old interrupting a speaking moment and questioning the "what-fors" of what I'm doing. Maybe it's just me, but don't the actions of the disciples sometimes strike you as childish, rather than mature?)*

Jesus responds by saying, "To you it has been granted to know the mysteries of the kingdom of heaven, but to them it has not been granted."[27]

Hmm, do you hear the rumbling noise of another Mac truck? This is big, ladies. Little did those puzzled disciples realize in their small, limited, finite minds that God had orchestrated every detail so as to make them part of the great Mystery. The minds of the Pharisees were closed due to unbelief; the minds of the disciples, while a bit slow in catching on sometimes *(I'd hate to think how long it might have taken me to "get" it)* would come to grasp every mystery—and spread everywhere the knowledge of Jesus in the years to come.

Jesus reveals the mystery of the Word of God:

"The seed is the Word of God. The seeds on the road are those who hear the Word, but no sooner do they hear it than the Devil snatches it from them so they won't believe and be saved. The seeds in the gravel are those who hear with enthusiasm, but the enthusiasm doesn't go very deep. It's only another fad, and the moment there's trouble it's gone. And the seed that fell in the weeds—well, these are the ones who hear, but then the seed is crowded out and nothing comes of it as they go about their lives worrying about tomorrow, making money, and having fun. But the seed in the good earth— these are the good-hearts who seize the Word and hold on no matter what, sticking with it until there's a harvest."[28]

And Paul tells us of a fabulous mystery revealed—but we can't talk about that until a later chapter, so hold on.

Clearly God enjoys revealing himself to us through his written message, the life of Jesus Christ, his Son, and the gentle promptings of the Holy Spirit. In fact, it is the Holy Spirit whom Jesus sent as a Helper to each of us. The Spirit, by his divine nature, is specially equipped to reveal truth to our soul.

"But when He, the Spirit of truth, comes, He will guide you into all the truth; for He will not speak on His own initiative, but whatever He hears, He will speak; and He will disclose to you what is to come. He will glorify Me; for He will take of Mine and will disclose it to you. All things that the Father has are Mine; therefore I said that He takes of Mine, and will disclose it to you."[29]

Who knows? Perhaps you can help someone else solve The Mystery!

Sweet Dreams Are Made of This

$\mathcal{I}$t was the summer of my discontent.

Sorta.

It was 1983, and the summer of the British musical invasion of The Eurythmics and one *highly* androgynous Annie Lennox. Perhaps it was not so much discontent I felt as much as I was dreaming of the things I wished could be.

Every evening during those warm summer months I routinely hoped for one of two things to happen. And since most of my hoping eventually wraps up in praying, here's what it sounded like those many years ago:

> *Dear God,*
>
> *Please let me wake up with hair as long as Cindy Crawford's. Dear God, please let Steve Perry notice me at the Journey concert in Kansas City, then want to meet me, ask me out for a date, and propose marriage.*

I was undeterred in my hey-it-could-happen dreams, despite using Clairol's Short and Sassy shampoo on my short-and-sassy hairstyle or the numerical reality of Steve Perry being old enough to be my father.

Each morning, following the previous night's request for luxurious flowing tresses, I'd wake up, keep my eyes shut, and bring myself to a sitting position on the edge of my bed. Then I'd turn toward the dresser mirror and, with full faith and expectation, simultaneously bring my hands to my shoulders *(as if to feel those flowing locks)* and open my eyes. As shocking as it may be, no flowing tresses ever greeted me. Just the same Pat Benatar-esque coiffure morning after morning.

And about my dream regarding Mr. Perry? Well, with overpriced ticket in hand one summer evening, I entered the halls of Kemper Arena with Cindy, Shelly, Jennifer, Lynda, Gerry Ann, and 48,994 other fans *(75 percent being female fans praying the exact same prayer).* Disregard the fact I was sitting, oh, let's say, six miles from the main stage. And factor in that I was 16 and, yeah, a might bit clueless. But I never let go of my hopeful belief that Steve *could* possibly see me, *could* possibly call me to the stage *(just as The Boss would in his "Dancing in the Dark" music video with Courtney Cox the following year),* and then *could* possibly fall madly in love with me, propose, and want to live forever in marital rock-and-roll harmony with me, Julie Ann Patrick.

Hey, a girl can always dream.

So what's the craziest thing you've ever dreamed would happen? And please, oh, please, tell me it was something shallow like the story I just shared.

Really, I mean it. If you were staying up late at night dreaming of world peace and global unity, well, I don't even want to know about it. And may I add, in my defense, that voluptuous hair and rock-and-roll bad boys weren't the only things on my mind that year. I did think once or twice about colleges I hoped to attend, occupations I hoped to aspire to *("Writer" coming in somewhere around #739 on the list, by the way)*, as well as more ethereal longings for relational, spiritual, and emotional connection with God, family, and friends.

Anyway, we all want something to hope for, regardless of our beliefs. Hope is what drives us in our continuing venture of attaining life, liberty, and the pursuit of happiness. Anybody who's anybody hopes for something. But it's *what* we hope for that distinguishes one from the other. And it is our dreams that often reveal the hope we are anchoring our past, present, and future to. Now I realize that hoping to marry the lead singer of a hard-living rock-and-roll band is not as noble as, say, hoping to live a long healthy life, or finding success in some form of business, or actually doing Bible devotions faithfully for more than nine days in a row. But at the time, voluptuous hair and Steve Perry were what seemed most important. *(Scary, huh?)*

So what's important enough for you to dream about? And please don't overspiritualize this question. If your first response has to do with things heavenly and noble—fine. If it's more along the lines of miraculous weight loss or radical overnight changes to your bust size—well, it is what it is, sister.

Remember, we're relaxing on this trip, so don't throw your brain out of whack trying to come up with something. Just mellow out and let those warm ocean currents and sandy ocean shores lull you back, as it were, to a place of dreamer's remembrance. . . .

Are you there yet? Good, and so are a few other women before you. Here's what they had to say when I asked their thoughts on hopes and dreams:

✳ I hope to create a home filled with things that make me smile. —BRITTANY, 15

✳ I've always dreamed of owning a horse. There's something about the details involved in its grooming, as well as the training needed to ride properly, that I believe would give me a great sense of accomplishment and worth. —TINA, 22

✳ Fasten your seat belt. Here's my number-one dream and number-one hope: I want to believe that God is real. And I also want to have faith to believe there really is such a place as heaven. I "hope" I get in. —RACHELLE, 42

✳ I've always held on to the dream that I would somehow grow more intellectually—that I'd just get smarter somehow. I find it embarrassing to talk with certain people because I just don't get things like they do. I feel stupid. My hope is that this feeling will go away eventually. But I'm still waiting. —LYDIA, 31

✳ I hope my children will love and take care of me the older I get. —MARGIE, 68

If I've learned anything over the course of nearly 40 years of existence, it is to never discount the power and promise of our dreams. It's been said that the eyes are the windows to the soul, but I say bookshelves run a close second. Bookshelves provide a plateglass view into what our hopes and dreams truly are made of. So I want you to do something for me. With this book in hand, grab a pad of paper, a pen, and go to wherever your books are located.

If you're like me, a few are actually on a bookshelf, while the rest *(the large majority)* are either stacked, piled, amassed, heaped, loaded, mounded, and/or stockpiled on or in various landings, tabletops, stairwells, end tables, or speakers. Some *(gasp)* may even be stored in basement boxes. But wherever they are located, get there with pen and paper! I'll be waiting. . . .

✳ ✳ ✳

Are you there? I'd like you to survey the dust jackets and spines of your books. Write down *(if you don't, you'll forget—trust me)* only the titles you have truly loved.

DO NOT include books you have rolled your eyes about and thought, *Puleeezze! My six-year-old could write a better story than this!*

DO NOT include books you have used as doorstops or props to hold up broken windows. Or ones you've placed spine out in a strategic place simply to impress your next-door neighbor.

DO NOT list any books you have not read but have been told were really good.

This little exercise may take a little while, and that's okay. I don't want you to rush through this because it really is important for you to list the books that have carved hope, possibility, identity, belonging, and change upon your life. So:

DO include titles that have caused you to long for the impossible.

DO list the books that have left you dumbfounded with empathetic grief.

DO, by all means, include any and all books that have dog-eared pages. The ones you've highlighted, underscored, quoted, and offered to others with equal parts of awe and worship.

Keep looking, keep writing, and as you do, categorize your said titles. You don't have to get fancy or anything. Simply follow basic shelving categories you might find at your local bookstore or public library. For instance, your largest percentage of favored titles may fall under the following categories: Nonfiction, Christian Spirituality, Apologetics, and Reference Studies.

Those are the categories my books break down into, at least. You won't find many copies of Historical Romance—I've never much liked reading about virile pirates and buxom, kidnapped damsels in distress *(or perhaps that should read: damsels being undressed)*. Neither will you find books covering such subject matter as Auto Repair, the Law of Physics *(wasn't that a syndicated television program or something?),* Poetry, or Computer Science/Programming *(I just figured out how to put page numbers on my Word documents a little over two years ago).* You will, however, find all manner of titles that could be grouped together under the category of Relationships.

I have books telling me how to be a better friend, writer, daughter, wife, daughter-in-law, Christian, speaker, neighbor, aunt, mother *(lots and lots of these!),* as well as how to fix my friends, fix my daughter, fix my husband, fix my in-laws, fix other Christians who really bug me, fix other speakers who go over their time restraints and leave me with four minutes to complete a 60-minute presentation, and fix my mother. Whew! I could open my own distribution center with these titles alone. There are all those titles, as well as the memory of books read to me at home and during Story Hour at the Brunswick Public Library. Add to that books discovered in musty bookshelves at my grandparents' and seized from imminent destruction at five-cent yard sales.

Whether your personal library consists of 20 titles or 2,500, I believe you'll soon spot a pattern of interest, and that's why I'm excited about you taking the time to do this. I believe reading interests often reveal to us *(and others)* the deepest longings of our heart. I believe the books we most consistently are drawn to purchase, borrow, and read *(as well as those I am compelled to write)* act as a conduit for this crazy little thing called hope.

One of the first books I can remember my mother reading to me was *Arthur and the Golden Guinea.* It was about a young English lad who lost a golden coin and then set about finding it. The illustrations weren't all that wonderful *(I noticed such things even then),* and I think my mom had to explain a guinea being a form of currency, rather than a feathered bird with sharp claws as I first believed, fairly early in our reading. Nevertheless, the overall moral of the story managed to stay with me all these years.

And then there was the original story of *The Boxcar Children.* Oh, how I loved that book! Read to me by my second-grade teacher, Dorothy Glenn, I was captivated by the four industrious orphans who managed to care for themselves and loved and cared for one another with sibling zeal. I admired the oldest child, Henry, who stepped up to the plate and found a job in order to provide milk and other necessities for his three younger siblings. My seven-year-old heart admired the protective and maternal instincts of Jessie and Violet, and I willed myself to be as adorable as six-year-old Benny.

A couple of years later, I was up to my eyeballs in Pippi Longstocking books. What 10-year-old couldn't or wouldn't love a character who ate as much chocolate as she liked when she liked, kept a pet horse on her back porch, and paid for life's certain expenses with gold coins safely "banked" in the trunk of a tree?

In my early teens I couldn't keep my hands or mind off an original memorial edition of a 1912 book titled *Sinking of the Titanic: Thrilling Stories Told by Survivors,* which I had discovered in my parents' home one rainy, spring day. The tattered and yellowed front and back covers and crinkled, dry pages threatened to crumble each time I held the book and read the true stories of heroes and cowards—the living and the dead. And it was the dead, or more specifically, the *listing* of the dead, that drew me back the most.

You see, it's one thing to read, "2,224 People Lose Their Lives," but another matter entirely to read the first, middle, and last names of each of those 2,224. Each name represented a man or woman, boy or girl, who had laughed as I had, shared meals with loved ones, and embarked on a journey across the sea with high hopes and thoughtful expectation. The horror that awaited each of them was almost more than I could take. In fact, I could only read the stories little by little, gentle dose by gentle dose. My empathetic 13-year-old heart could only bear so many tales of anguish and loss.

As I survey my titles, those are the books that truly captured my heart. The ones that now reveal my God-given longings and dreams.

In *Arthur and the Golden Guinea* I was struck by the promise that, with due diligence, you *can* recover things that were once lost. I was maybe four or five years old when I first heard those written words, yet the longing of recovering lost things had already been indelibly branded on my heart and memory. Even then, barely out of toddlerhood, I held on to the dream of one day finding the sisters I had lost through adoption. That child-like faith —coupled with what I believe to be God-given hope[1] and *it-could-happen* dreaming—kept me believing, kept me *hoping* for years and years to come.

Pippi Longstocking, with her gravity-defying pigtails, convinced me there wasn't a thing wrong with being a bit kooky. In fact, I distinctly recall choosing to be more, um, *unique* after reading of her adventures in the South Seas. Pippi faced the world with unflappable ease, had a tender heart the size of Texas, missed her deceased mother, and ached to know about her father who was rumored to have been lost at sea.

Hmm . . . it doesn't take a rocket scientist to figure out why I was drawn to this story! Like its title character, I mourned *(with equal brave outer face)* the loss of family and desired to find answers to varied rumors and doubt. Like Pippi *(in fact, it's the very reason I wanted to be more like Pippi)*, I longed to know the truth regarding my birth mother and birth father who, for all intents and purposes, seemed dead or lost at sea.

It was this loss, this same restlessness, that made my heart tender and kept me sensitive to others' grief.

I'm not sure a 13-year-old who had remained in her family of origin, or who had never witnessed siblings being broken apart, or questioned why she couldn't get straight answers to fairly simple questions would have responded to the *Titanic* list of victims quite the way I did. The tales of *Titanic* and the list of her dead confronted my sense of loss and my dream of belonging—of being a person of value—to someone who loved me. *(And oh, how my adopted parents loved me . . . yet still I dreamed of what it would have been like to live with my birth family. How would my life have been different?)*

Looking back now, it's somewhat startling to see just how characters, words, sometimes fictional circumstances, and true tales of survival, could provide unlimited dreams of the impossible for my soul, mind, and heart. But they did. You see, each book I mentioned presented, in one form or another, a child who was quite self-sufficient—yet longed for interdependence with others. Each book presented a child or children who found themselves orphaned—and never stopped hungering for a place of belonging. And each book tapped into the almost primal wish for . . . *hope*. Even as young as age four, I had that wish for finding what I had lost and powerfully missed.

After I did my own book survey, I came to realize how strongly God uses books to speak to the intrinsic divine notations of what we believe and what we feel in the deepest recess of our soul. For it is in the deep places of longing for what was, what is, and what may be that the overarching themes of story and verse often find their way. And they'll reveal to us, if we'll listen, our sadness of dreams thwarted.

C. S. Lewis aptly notes such power:

*A*lready in our schooldays some of us were making our first responses to good literature. Others, and these the majority, were reading at school, The Captain, and at home, short-lived novels from the circulating library. But it was apparent then that the majority did not "like" their fare in the way we "liked" ours. It is apparent still. The differences leap to the eye.

In the first place, the majority never read anything twice. The sure mark of the unliterary man is that he considers "I've read it already" to be a conclusive argument against reading a work. . . . Those who read great works, on the other hand, will read the same work ten, twenty, or thirty times during the course of their life.

*S*econdly, the majority, though they are sometimes frequent readers, do not set much store by reading. They turn to it as a last resource. They abandon it with alacrity as soon as any alternative pastime turns up. . . . [But] literary people are always looking for leisure and silence in which to read and do so with their whole attention. When they are denied such attentive and undisturbed reading even for a few days they feel impoverished.

*T*hirdly, the first reading of some literary work is often, to the literary, an experience so momentous that only experiences of love, religion, or bereavement can furnish a standard of comparison. *Their whole consciousness is changed. They have become what they were not before* [italics mine]. But there is no sign of anything like this among the other sort of readers. When they have finished the story or the novel, nothing much, or nothing at all, seems to have happened to them.[2]

All right, how many of you were nearly jumping up and down

upon reading the italicized portion of Mr. Lewis's comments?
I began crying the first time I surveyed those glorious sentences
and thoughts. I had finally found *(though I never consciously
knew I was looking)* someone who articulated what had been
occurring in my heart and mind with books.

Truth is, I'd always considered my all-consuming love of
books, as well as the accompanying emotional and spiritual
bonds I made with them, to be part of an overall weirdness that
no one would ever understand. But hey, it turns out there *are*
people like me after all. Yes, indeed, what an odd pairing I had
made with Pippi, C. S. Lewis, and myself.

As I read *(again and again and again)* these words, *"Their
whole consciousness is changed. They have become what they
were not before,"* I am convinced all the more of God's great
passion toward us. I am convinced of his eclectic style of com-
municating, as well as the eternal truth that he is continually at
work, revealing his desire for our lives through our whole and
yes, even our broken, dreams.

It doesn't surprise me a bit that he would choose to use writ-
ers and books to expose our most tender longings for hope—
after all, he's been doing just that for quite a few years now.
Remember my asking in Chapter 1 if hope was something you
had to ask for or if somehow you just got it *(kind of like those
free packets of laundry detergent that arrive in the mail every now
and then)*? I've mulled it over for some time now and have come
to the following wise conclusion: Hope is a little bit of this and a
little bit of that.

Read the following promise of hope and tell me what you
think.

"This is God's Word on the subject: '. . . I'll show up and take care of you as I promised and bring you back home. I know what I'm doing. I have it all planned out—plans to take care of you, not abandon you, plans to give you the future you hope for.'"[3]

It seems God is clearly the giver of any and all desires and dreams we would label as hope. And some of you have no doubt heard or quoted those familiar verses from the Old Testament book of Jeremiah. But let's not stop there. Let's keep reading and see what we might uncover regarding the divine work of hope.

"When you call on me, when you come and pray to me, I'll listen. When you come looking for me, you'll find me. Yes, when you get serious about finding me and want it more than anything else, I'll make sure you won't be disappointed."[4]

Wow! I honestly don't recall hearing these accompanying verses quoted along with verse 11. How eye-opening it is to read that God, who is actively involved in every aspect of creation[5] and has nothing but the best in mind for our future, expressly reveals his intent and desire for each of us to participate and seek out his leadership in our life-long quest for hope.

A little bit of this *(God)* and a little bit of that *(concentrated intent),* indeed!

But what about our dreams that have come to naught?

What about the raw, ragged sorrow propelling us to run from, rather than rest in, God and the Anchor of our soul?

What do you do when you find yourself wanting nothing more

but to pack up those dreams, pitch them in a garbage bag, throw them out alongside the curb, and bid them good riddance? Yet you know if you do so, you're trashing your very soul as well.

What do we do with hearts that are restless?

We do the only thing we can do, ladies. We run, we jog, we limp, we crawl, we cry out to The One who made us. And he will find us, hear us, and heal us. This isn't some trite little Christian statement I'm throwing on the page as filler. Anne Lamott said it best: "Hope begins in the dark, the stubborn hope that if you just show up and try to do the right thing, the dawn will come."[6] There's nothing simple, or easy, or necessarily "spiritual feeling" about showing up. Sometimes it takes everything that you have *(which isn't much on some days, I know)*. But if you will, God will never leave you lonely.

Never.

If we were gathered together in my living room talking, I'd tell you why I know this to be true. I'd tell you all the gory details of feeling as if my heart was going to burst through my chest as I spoke one afternoon with a counselor and tried to staunch the flood of agonizing sorrow and loss. I'd tell you how I prayed, *God, don't let me throw up!* as I came to grips with the depth of my grief and found it nearly impossible to move.

How do you mend a broken heart? How do you deal with broken dreams and loss?

You simply show up for the next moment.

And the next.

And the next.

And the next.

Funny how in the face of profound sorrow you can think of the goofiest things. My mind goes back to Mrs. Carol Edmundson's second-grade music class. We were all gathered *(12 strong, mind you)* in a glorious room filled with a full-size piano, stringed instruments, tambourines *(the only item I could ever play somewhat on beat)*, and items from our past Christmas program.

I thought Mrs. Edmundson was the prettiest teacher in the entire school, and I would have done anything for her *(even sat next to Merle Warren if she asked)*. On this particular day she was excited about introducing a new song. Just the other week we had learned "Music, Music, Music," and she told us we'd enjoy this one even more. I couldn't wait, so I quickly raised my hand and volunteered to pass out the lyrics as she pushed the stand-up piano slowly around to face us.

She agreed to let me do so. While I handed out 12 sheets of paper with the song title "High Hopes" mimeographed somewhat blurrily across the top, I began to smile. I was an optimist even then, and I just knew the song had to be good with a title like that.

Sitting down, Mrs. Edmundson then instructed us to listen as she played and sang through the first verse. She had me with "ant and rubber tree plant"! Before too long, 12 enthusiastic seven-year-olds were bellowing the first and second refrains—especially enjoying the second as we were allowed to sing *(with gusto)* a word that rhymed with *ram.* She had us all believing that anything was possible, as long as you dreamed it and kept working toward it.

That silly song wafted through my memory the day I was experiencing a nuclear meltdown with my counselor. On my way back home, I began humming it through my tears. Just what makes this silly woman think she can deal with a few hundred thwarted dreams? Just what keeps her keeping on even when she wants to give up, in, out, and over already? Anytime I feel like letting go, what do I hold to? The Hope of Christ and of the Creator, who tells me he knows my name, he knows my every need, and I will find my rest—here and forever—in him alone.

Sweet dreams *are* made of this.

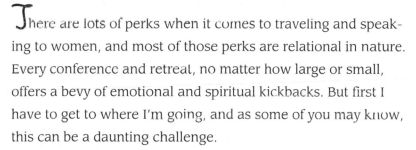

* 4 *

How Are You . . . Really?

There are lots of perks when it comes to traveling and speaking to women, and most of those perks are relational in nature. Every conference and retreat, no matter how large or small, offers a bevy of emotional and spiritual kickbacks. But first I have to get to where I'm going, and as some of you may know, this can be a daunting challenge.

What with books and notes to gather, clothes and shoes to pack, a car to park *(and to remember where I parked it—always a bonus),* and flight itineraries to track, well, I'm generally teetering on collapse before I even make it through the first block of security pat downs. *(Oh, let me give you another heads-up regarding metal and said security measures: DO NOT under any fashion or cellulite circumstances wear a one-piece body shaper with metal front closures. It's not pretty, girls—that's all I'm saying.)*

So, given my past track record and my future calendar loaded with travel dates, I thought it best if I finally took the plunge and hired an assistant—an apprentice, so to speak, but hopefully one who showed far less cleavage than any of Donald Trump's wannabes. Remember, however, that I grew up as an only child and that I'm somewhat opinionated and a tad bit controlling. And while a lover of spending time with people, I also like to have my own space.

Hmm, seems like any apprentice would have their work cut out for them, right?

Add to that the fact that while I have traveled fairly regularly over the past few years, I've spent little one-on-one time with anyone save my husband. Look, I've been married nearly 18 years, so this is a *very* big deal. Rick and I have that certain travel familiarity that one can quickly take for granted. You see, we don't have to explain ourselves to one another or apologize for our individual pathologies.

For instance, my husband knows I don't like to have my shoulders massaged by him or any other person on the face of the earth. My shoulders are not a ball of dough begging to be kneaded, and rather than relaxing me *(as is the magnanimous intent of all self-appointed massagers)*, massaging brings out the more tense and prickly nature of an otherwise docile personality.

My husband knows I must immediately *(as in tip the doorman, latch the safety lock, open the suitcase, expel all contents)* set all personal items on the bathroom vanity as to create a sense of home in an otherwise bland and impersonal hotel room. He also knows all items must then be arranged in an orderly, tallest to shortest, fashion.

My husband knows the bathroom is my library away from home, and I have first dibs on the LIFE section of *USA Today. (News isn't "new" if someone has read it before me.)*

My husband knows I blow up like a Kool-Aid *(Blackberry*

Splash, to be specific) puffer fish after consuming any form of shrimp.

And he also knows I still break out in random *(but far less than before, thanks to Nasonex)* moments of chainsaw snoring and yet still finds me attractive in the morning. Er, make that attractive and approachable after a brush of Colgate and splash of Chanel No. 5, that is.

This is how we function. Better said, this is how he knows I function. So it was with more than a bit of trepidation that I embarked on the assistant quest. This woman was going to have to be one kind of a trouper.

I thought I had a keeper with Lori Havens. She was a go-getter, unafraid to fly *(always a plus when 99 percent of your time together will be spent hurtling through air via jet),* and she knew me well enough to not be impressed in the least. Her sister was the mother of my oldest son's best friend, and as such, Lori knew exactly how things went in the Barnhill family household. Exactly.

On our first day together in my "office" *(the cluttered space in the basement of my home, built in 1927),* Lori set to organizing shelves and making better use of my limited resources. Three hours later I could find my mailing envelopes. I could walk across the cold concrete floor and not trip over stacks of resource material *(a.k.a., People magazines, a 2003 Coach purse catalog, and a box of Russell Stover's butternut toffee sticks).* I was thrilled and couldn't wait until our first trip together—then, alas, a full-time employment position called her name.

So I waited and hoped for someone who would be able to put up with me and, more importantly, understand the awesome privilege of meeting women and being a part of their lives. It took her all of two weeks to show up.

While speaking at an event in Rushville, Illinois, I renewed a minor acquaintance with a woman who had worked with my husband 10 years previous. Kathy Drake had organized the weekend women's event and surprised me with her command of the stage even when giving simple announcements. We talked and prayed a bit during the day and as I left for home, I thought out loud, "Now there's someone I think I could enjoy working with."

A few days later she phoned and, in the middle of our conversation, I blurted out, "Kathy, would you ever consider traveling with me as an assistant?"

There was a brief *(brief! Anyone who knows me knows I can't stand more than a second of silence on the phone or I break out in hives . . .)* moment of silence, then a squeal of laughter. "Oh, Julie! I was just telling my husband, Allen, how much I would love to travel with you and help you get things done *(had she noticed my pathologies a bit that weekend?).* And I would love to see God work in the lives of the women who come to your events."

A little bit of God, a little bit of purposeful intent, and voilà! In the midst of the chaos of what I do—as wife, mother, speaker, and encourager of women—God had provided a couple of wonderful perks that gave me hope for the daily grind.

PERK #1: AN ASSISTANT!

Thanks to God and Kathy, I now have someone who intrinsically knows how to best set up a display table. I have someone to bounce book ideas off of and someone to eat pizza with in my hotel room long after a meeting adjourns. I now enjoy a

low-maintenance business and a personal relationship that
never ceases to refresh my soul. We have, however, agreed to
stay in private rooms when traveling. Those pathologies really
can get on your nerves after so many trips! *(Come on, be honest—you've got them too.)*

Everyone needs a perk like Kathy. Maybe you don't need a
personal assistant. But all of us need a friend we can "tell all"
to because she knows and loves us unconditionally anyway.
And this is most important when Perk #2 comes along.

PERK #2: FABULOUS MOMENTS OF COMMUNICATION . . .
FOR THE GOOD AND THE BAD

As a result of so much time spent with meeting planners, atten-
dees of conferences, and readers of my books, I've enjoyed some
fabulous moments of communication. I love hearing from women
who have struggled and succeeded in love and life; motherhood
and work; faith and, well, moments of unbelief too. It's not
uncommon for me to receive 10 or 15 new e-mails each morning
or a phone call or two a day from women who want to tell me
what they've learned and how my words have encouraged them.

Therefore, I was in my usual relaxed reading mode three
years ago when I began reading the subject line and content
of this e-mail:

Subject: how are you . . . *really?*
From: a concerned friend
To: julie@juliebarnhill.com
Dear Julie,

I feel a little strange writing this note, but I just can't seem to shake
this sense of needing to do so. Last week I attended the conference you

were a part of and, while I enjoyed the sessions you taught, I was unable to concentrate on the subject matter you were teaching. All around me women were laughing, crying, taking notes, and whispering back and forth, "She is so like me."

But again, I couldn't seem to get into your message. There was something about you—maybe it was the tone of your voice or a look in your eyes. But as crazy as this may sound, I felt like God wanted me to "see" something and then encourage *(maybe challenge?)* you with it.

I came home thinking I was crazy. But I couldn't shake that feeling *(and by the way, I am so not a "feeling" type of woman)*. As I went to bed that night, I prayed that God would either show me what he wanted me to see or just leave me alone.

Well, I think you know how that prayer was answered. Here's what I believe God wanted me to see. Take or leave it. Believe me or write me off as a nutty, disgruntled conference attendee. But I write this knowing with unquestionable certainty that I am not crazy and it is real God stuff. *(That probably makes me sound even worse, doesn't it?)* Whatever— here's what I see. . . .

I see you running around, doing so many good things but running yourself ragged. I see you trying to do the right thing; teaching women about the scandalous love and grace of God; writing books with a voice of honesty seldom read in Christian women circles. But somehow you are losing hope in the midst of it all. God wants you to know you can let go of your restless heart.

He wants you to rest . . . physically and spiritually. Rest and know that he is God. You don't have to push for your own agenda or get everything "right" to have done things well. Trust in him to come through, Julie. And above all, don't lose hope!

So there you go. I guess you'll either hit "Delete" or maybe, just maybe, find this e-mail to be just the word of encouragement you need for today.

DIANA

A WAKE-UP CALL

If I'd ever received a wake-up call, this was it! I sat, stunned, as I read the e-mail. I did not delete Diana's message. Nor did I write her off as a wacko, disgruntled, conference attendee. No, I read her e-mail once, twice, and then again and again, finding myself drawn to her observations. *(And maybe, girls, you'll see yourself in some of them too, just as I did.)*

Doing so many good things but running yourself ragged. Truer words were never spoken. While generally a well-organized person, I was finding myself becoming overwhelmed by the never-ending lists of things to do. Each day there were airfare purchases to make, speaking inquiries to follow up on, writing outlines to tweak, and trip itineraries to confirm as I tried to keep track of my three children's school responsibilities and sports activities in the midst of it all. I was attempting to keep up with the housework, trying to keep my relationship with my husband interesting *(i.e., do something other than watch another episode of* Law & Order *together)* and, oh yeah, in case I found an additional minute of time, I tried to keep teaching a Bible study class. But because I was a Christian, I didn't want to sound like I was complaining about any of those things. After all, they were all good things to be doing and could be considered "blessings" from God.

So why then was I doing such a lousy job at all of them?

Let go of your restless heart.
When I read that phrase in the e-mail, I really winced. Again, truer words were never spoken. Somehow, deep within, I had managed again to place my significance and worth as a woman in yet one more false measurement. And to make things worse, this new false measurement was apart from any of the above-named items, for which I already felt guilty for failing in. I was suffering from a restless heart due to the mother of all measurement for the world as I knew it: book sales totals.

(Insert crazy Psycho *shower scene music here.)*

Just a few days before, I'd received the latest sales statement for my second book, *'Til Debt Do Us Part,* which is all about my own journey through financial failure and back. And I immediately felt like a different kind of failure—a loser of the most useless literary type. I had wondered about, even feared, the possibility the whole time I was writing my second book. Now my theory was officially confirmed: Julie Ann Barnhill was a one-hit writing flunky who should let her new publishing house, Tyndale, out of their just-signed contract, and should then go back to scrubbing bathroom baseboards with a toothbrush.

What a disappointing writer I turned out to be. I was over-shadowed by the weight of failure. Those low sales figures ate at my gut, at my confidence, at my life purpose, slowly eroding my hope for what I could do . . . what I could be.

You don't have to push for your own agenda.
Aha, that's why those low book-sale figures bothered me so much, I reasoned. You see, I'd always had a clear-cut idea of what I thought I should be doing before age 40. It's one of the reasons

I had my children in my early and mid-twenties, because that timing fit the overall plan I had for my life—love, marriage, children, a professional career, a minor degree of success, and then early retirement *(on an oceanside property, of course)*. And believe me, I was working it. I barely cleared the "I should be published before age 35" agenda. *She's Gonna Blow* was published in April 2001, when I was 34 years and nine months old. Whew!

However, any pride I may have felt regarding being the author of two books quickly vaporized as my agenda of "earning an income via writing" came to a screeching halt with the cold truth of the sales number on that second book. Naturally that led to starting a fresh agenda list for my life regarding public speaking, thus spinning my wheels faster and faster and putting the *rag* in *ragged* all the more. I might as well have been a hamster, stuck spinning on a wheel in a tiny cage. That's how trapped I felt! But I'd been so busy just staying on that wheel that I hadn't even noticed I was going nowhere, and I was getting pooped in the process.

You don't have to do everything "right" to have done things well.

Boy, did the gutsy Diana hit the nail on the head with that one. Little did she know *(or perhaps God had whispered that truth into her ear too?)* how I'd struggled during that conference weekend. I had wondered the whole time if I had prayed enough, prepared enough, or presented my thoughts with enough clarity to impact any woman's life whatsoever. See, as long as I've lived in the Land of Julie *(a very, very scary place)*, it has been and all

too often still is about doing, getting, being, preparing, and trying to do things right.

Right for Jesus, that is.

What exactly do I mean? So often *(unfortunately I can only see
this via hindsight—what about you?)* it isn't enough for me to
simply write, speak, mother, or teach a class. No, it is about me
doing *all* those things, doing them simultaneously *(the myth of
Superwoman is not dead), and* doing them in a way I believe is
right for the things of God—for his unchanging purpose in this
world. *(Yes, it's a heady thought but one I actually have on occasion. Or, perhaps, on too many occasions for my own good.)* If you
happen to have a personality like mine *(the plunge-in-and-do-
everything-at-once type),* the measure of doing things right spiritually often works hand and glove with having some outward
measure of success also. Otherwise, how do you know if you're
doing things *right* or not?

**Trust in him to come through, Julie. And above all, don't
lose hope!**

Diana's *(i.e., God's)* final thoughts were what meant the most to
me that day as I sat, head bowed, in front of my computer
screen.

Fact is, my heart—i.e., the whole person in all of my distinctive human activity as a thinking, planning, willing, feeling, wor-
shipping, socially interacting being—had become very restless
and had, in fact, lost hope. There were innumerable changes
and stresses in my personal life, budding professional endeav-
ors, and *(to be honest)* somewhat tepid spiritual development.
I'd appeared on *Oprah,* interviewed with Dr. Dobson, and was

actually booked several months in advance for speaking events. I suppose, from the outside, it looked like I had the Christian life nailed. But I knew—and more importantly, God knew—things were not as they appeared.

I was trying to do all the right things with all the changes in my life: limiting my travel away from home to two weekends a month; arranging a date night for Rick and me at least two times a month; alerting teachers to my travel schedule and keeping on top of my three children's school, social, and sporting calendars; continuing teaching a women's Bible study class on Sunday mornings; responding *personally* to each e-mail, letter, or phone call received; keeping track of outgoing expenses and shuffling money and bills *(quite a trick for me)* in as timely a manner as possible, etc.

Deep breath.

You and I both know this list could go on and on and on.

Then, in spite of my best intentions and plans, two weekends away quickly turned into three and four as I worried about Rick's future employment possibilities *(he'd returned to college to acquire his bachelor's degree in human resources)* and endeavored to squirrel away as much money as possible. It seemed like the right thing to do. Now, this may not be a big deal for some of you, but it was to me. You see, from 1988 until 2000, I had remained home full time with my kids, and the most income I had ever generated was a whopping $1,200 in 1994. So I found the role of wage earner to be good, invigorating, and slightly heady.

Too good, perhaps, for I looked forward more and more to those days away from home—away from responsibilities, mom stuff, and wife stuff—in order to find temporary *(and I do mean temporary)* rest in the busyness and perceived rightness of performance and ministry.

Of course, a lot of things didn't get done. *Or at least didn't get done as well as if I'd been there to oversee them,* I told myself. Homework assignments were missed, date nights didn't happen, and an overall disconnect formed between me and my family. The Sunday morning class was handed over more and more to a co-teacher *(we were to have shared responsibilities every other Sunday)* and when I did return home physically, My Mind tended not to follow. The e-mails mounted, along with my guilt. My juggling act faltered as bills and check balances took a fall. And the more I seemed to be doing for God, the further my heart seemed to be from him. Have you been there too, girlfriend? Are you there now?

Years ago I had written in a journal,

> When fame screams my name, whisper, "Jesus."
> When flattery cloaks the tongue, whisper, "Jesus."
> When hope seems lost, whisper, "Jesus."

Well, a certain level of notoriety had screamed my name and I had tried my best to whisper, "Jesus."

Flattery came a-knockin' as I repeated time and time again, "It's not about you, Julie, it's not about you." *(Too bad I didn't draw that little concept up into a book proposal at the time. It might have stuck earlier and caused a lot less pain in my life!)* But hope faltered, uttered one gasp, and began to flatline as I saw the ever-widening gap between me and the people I truly cared about.

That was the certain "something" that God allowed Diana to see, for God used her to show that he knew all about me and cared beyond anything I could ever imagine. And, ladies, he cares the same for you.

HOPE FOR A RESTLESS HEART

Diana asked me, and now I ask you: "How are you . . . *really?*" It's a question that unlatches a door, but it's up to each of us to decide whether to pull that door open or allow it to remain closed.

But one thing I know for sure: We were never created to go it alone, ladies. If we attempt to face life's complexities alone, our heart and hope will shrivel. God has created us for community—for belonging. We'll talk about this more in the next chapter. For now I ask you to consider this suggestion: When you share your pain and others acknowledge their care for you, then hope begins to grow. A hope that is eternal and not based on day-to-day circumstances. A hope that aids a restless heart

The truth is, all of us will have restless hearts as long as we sojourn on this earth. It's part of the human story. Even the great St. Augustine admitted his own restlessness boldly in the beginning of his *Confessions:* "You have made us for yourself, O Lord, and our hearts are restless until they rest in you."[1] He reminded his readers just how fleeting experiences—such as gaining wealth, indulging in bodily pleasures, and acquiring glory and power—can be, no matter how good they might be and feel in themselves. And he stated that lasting happiness can neither be found nor guaranteed in external possessions. He also revealed a secret that helps put things in perspective for me: God allows us to have this "restless" feeling to show us that earth is not our final destination.

The esteemed C. S. Lewis agreed:

*I*f I find in myself a desire which no experience in this world can satisfy, the most probable explanation is that I was made for another world.[2]

So in this life we are pilgrims, wanderers who cannot stay on earth permanently even if we wanted to. (And who would really want to? *I ask, especially in my most exhausted moments.* Take me away, Lord! *I cry.*)

Yes, our hearts will be restless until they rest eternally in God. Until we see Jesus Christ as both the highway and the goal of our journey. And until we see, with our own eyes, our glorious destination of heaven.

A king of Israel once wrote,

"*W*hy are you in despair, O my soul? And why have you become disturbed within me? Hope in God, for I shall again praise Him for the help of His presence."[3]

If you find yourself in a similar place—the place of despair and emotional trauma—as this king of old, be encouraged. You are not alone, and God is not far off from you. In fact, stop and give thanks for the restlessness of your soul. *(Uh, yes, I am serious.)* Really, without such restlessness, we would not even seek God or find the hope that can carry us through the difficult times.

Sigmund Freud believed that hope was an illusion. But I

have seen proof, within my own life, of how wrong Freud was. Hope is a longing woven into the very DNA construct of every human by their Creator. And our restless wanderings and heart longings are what he uses to remind us of him . . . and what is to come.

As C. S. Lewis says so aptly in *Mere Christianity*:

Ɔf none of my earthly pleasures satisfy it, that does not prove that the universe is a fraud. Probably earthly pleasures were never meant to satisfy it, but only to arouse it, to suggest the real thing. If that is so, I must take care, on the one hand, never to despise, or be unthankful for, these earthly blessings, and on the other, never to mistake them for the something else of which they are only a kind of copy, or echo, or mirage. I must keep alive in myself the desire for my true country, which I shall not find till after death; I must never let it get snowed under or turned aside; I must make it the main object of life to press on to that other country and to help others do the same.[4]

So is our desiring to be a good mother, a loving wife, a success-ful writer, a financially savvy businesswoman *(or anything else)* wrong or displeasing to God? Certainly not. In fact, we are told, "Whatever you do in word or deed, do all in the name of the Lord Jesus, giving thanks through Him to God the Father."[5] Doing is good. But when we try to quiet our restlessness of soul by getting caught up in the work of life *(the "copy, or echo, or mirage" as C. S. Lewis says)*, we lose our way.

Girlfriend, what have you done or thought or used to quiet your heart's restlessness? Is it working for the long haul? Only you can answer that question.

But what I do know is this: My own heart and its ability to hope in God and rest in hope are inevitably linked. How often I need the reminder of Scripture:

"Don't love the world's ways. Don't love the world's goods. Love of the world squeezes out love for the Father. Practically everything that goes on in the world—wanting your own way, wanting everything for yourself, wanting to appear important—has nothing to do with the Father. It just isolates you from him. The world and all its wanting, wanting, wanting is on the way out—but whoever does what God wants is set for eternity."[6]

We all want something—be it success, stature, a child, or true connection in marriage. We all want . . . and yet we're never satisfied with those things alone. As soon as one desire is fulfilled or met, two more spring into our mind. And so it goes.

So, my friend, "How are you . . . *really?*"

God desires for us to find completion in him alone.

* 5 *

Ɗt's the Small Things

Ɗn spring 2004 I traveled with friends Becky Wiese and Brenda Paccamonti to the European countries of Austria, Hungary, and England.

There was a minor itinerary change in Chicago upon our arrival *("I'm sorry, your flight to Amsterdam has been canceled, but we can get you on a jet to Brussels if you can make it to the international boarding gate in, oh, six minutes.")*

And a major seatmate issue for the 14-hour ride to Brussels. *(The man sitting three centimeters to my right had horrendously bad breath. And why do I know this? Because he breathed through his mouth for the entire 14 hours! And there was a reason for the wheezing, girls. He was reading a paperback of ill repute—hey, I saw the cover. It's kind of hard to miss at three centimeters. Nice, real nice).*

Upon our arrival we were met by Karen Dossett *(a native of Illinois now working with her husband, Mark, as a missionary in Vienna)* and it was official: We were the 2004 travel team for Hearts at Home, Inc., a nondenominational, Christ-centered, professional organization for mothers at home or those who want to be.

During our 13 days of travel, it was my responsibility and pleasure to lead a women's Bible study in the picturesque town of Guntramsdorf, Austria, where only two or three of the participants spoke or understood English. I also acted as keynote speaker for our Saturday morning "Mom's Morning Out" program in Vienna and moderated a roundtable discussion after a lunch with participants.

The four of us also traveled to the former communist city of Budapest, Hungary, where we met with Linda and Patti— two women keen on bringing the Hearts at Home message to mothers in Budapest. It was exhilarating, to say the least, and a trip that screamed of hope throughout each and every minute.

One in particular . . .

✳   ✳   ✳

It was the morning of our Saturday program in Vienna, and I was attempting to help Becky and Brenda the best I could. But given the fact I had scored 0 on an administrative abilities test some years earlier, it didn't surprise me, or them, that I was far less dangerous and much more useful as a greeter.

So I was meeting and greeting when two women approached me. One was smiling broadly, and the other had the most startling green eyes I had ever seen. Immediately I felt myself drawn to the second woman. Now that may sound sappy—or even a bit melodramatic—but it's true. There was something . . .

a connection of the soul . . . that made me quickly decide I'd like to get to know this green-eyed woman in particular.

I had just given them an American welcome hug when the smiling woman asked, "Do you know a woman named Lana Barnhill?"

"Well, I certainly do! She's married to my husband's first cousin."

Smiling even broader, the woman added, "Well, Lana is one of my closest friends. My husband and I used to live in Peoria, Illinois, and we knew Lana and her husband, Jimmy, really well. My name is Shelly."

Get out! What were the chances, after surviving a smelly flight to Brussels, of me running into a woman who had once lived less than 60 miles from my home in the States? And what were the chances she would know a relative's wife? Go figure.

But it gets even better. A second or so later, Shelly introduced me to her green-eyed friend, Renata, who immediately leaned in toward me and said, "Julie, I was hoping you could ride with Shelly and me to the luncheon after the meeting. I really feel as if I should talk with you."

I felt the same. It was the "connection" thing, and I assured her we would find time to do just that.

A few hours later I sat across from her at lunch and we talked. Better still, Renata talked and I listened. I learned she had been born and raised in Berlin while it was still under Communist rule, but she had grown up in a religious home. She had attended church until her 18th birthday, when she felt she was old enough to choose what she believed and if she needed the church. Her decision had been to opt out for a while.

I had just begun to ask her some questions regarding matters of faith when our lunches arrived. Our conversation paused while we both enjoyed authentic Wiener schnitzel.

Soon after, all the women in attendance (about 22) gathered their chairs in a circle as we opened the format to questions and comments regarding motherhood, faith, life, and anything in between.

Despite sincere, yet pitiful, pronunciation skills of the German language on my part and thanks to the superb translation skills of Becky and Greta, a woman sitting next to me, we all somehow managed to talk. And talk long enough that the women's cell phones began ringing with frantic messages from homebound husbands asking, "When are you coming back home to the children!?"

I was just about ready to wrap things up when Renata spoke up. "Julie," she began, "I have been sitting here listening to you and some of the other women talk about this faith in Jesus Christ. I have always wondered what this meant. My husband, who is a physicist, tells me there is no God. He says the world is simply made up of atoms and energy. And yet I listen to you, and I wonder, *Is that all there really is?*"

You could have heard a pin drop. Every woman of faith recognized the holiness of that moment.

Renata drew in a breath and continued, "You see, Julie, I don't really think that much about God. Quite honestly, when things are good, I do not think of him at all. But when things are bad, I wonder why he would let something like this happen to me. Where is he?"

All eyes were turned to Renata, who had dared to express her deepest thoughts to a patio of strangers *(she and Shelly had driven close to four hours to attend the Hearts at Home event).* I quickly looked at Brenda, who was smiling *(and I knew praying)* as I groped for just the right words to say.

"Renata," I said, capturing her straightforward gaze, "you have just summed up the entire experience of humankind. We all question the reality of God. And I believe we do that because God himself placed that curiosity within us. Why would he do that? Because he wants to make himself *known* to us. I believe, with all my heart, that there is a God, and that he longs for you to know all there is to know about him. When your husband tells you the world is made up of atoms and energy, he's right. It is indeed. But all the atoms and all the energy contained within them is the result of God's creation. There is One who holds all things together, Renata, and his name is Jesus Christ."[1] Just then another cell phone began to ring, and the hallowed moment was quickly broken. Women began gathering their possessions and saying their good-byes as I walked over toward Shelly and Renata.

As I reached this beautiful, green-eyed woman, I cupped my hands gently around her face. I spoke directly into her eyes and hopefully her heart: "Renata, the next time you wonder if there is a God, I want you to think about some seemingly 'small things.'"

Her eyes were questioning as I went on.

"Think about Shelly's husband being transferred to Europe a little over a year ago.

"Think about you and Shelly somehow meeting in a city full of hundreds of thousands of people and discovering that certain 'click' that forms a friendship.

"Think about the time you have spent with Shelly since you first met and how she knew how important it would be for you to attend an event that encouraged you as a mother.

"Think how you were both able to juggle family responsibilities in such a way as to be here.

"Think about the fact that God put together friendships and contacts in the United States and Austria over 10 years ago to make this event possible today.[2]

"Think about the fact that Shelly knows one of my extended family members.

"Think about the fact that God brought a specific woman speaker from the United States to be here on this day, and you instantly felt compelled to speak with her. And she felt the same toward you."

By this point Shelly was tearing up, Renata was hugging me fiercely, and I was ready to pack my bags, hop in their car, and head home with them as I finished with these words: "Renata, there are answers to the questions and longings you so bravely expressed to each of us. I believe the same Jesus who holds atoms and energy together also organized each and every 'small thing' that made this day possible. And I believe he did it so that you might know he's absolutely *crazy* about you and he wants you to know all this was for *you!* For you to know that he exists—and he is more than willing to answer your questions."

Then, grabbing my Bible, I asked Renata to write her name and address on its pages so I might be able to keep in touch. I placed it on the table, and as I did, she looked down incredulously and asked, "Is this a real Bible?"

When I nodded yes, she said, "It has been so long. . . ." It hit me that because she'd grown up in an Eastern Bloc country, even her "religious family" probably wasn't allowed to have a Bible.

I don't think I have ever seen an expression such as hers. She touched the pages of my Bible with an awe and reverence that shamed me *(think back to Annie Dillard's observation in Chapter 3)* and made me make an immediate, internal note to make sure that she somehow received a Bible of her own.

"Yes it is," I replied. "I sort of use mine as a journal too—I write down prayers and questions and problems I'm having, and I also make a note of prayers answered. My life from age 18 to today is in this Bible. Now you will be in my Bible, and every time I see your name written on the pages of Jeremiah, chapter 52, page 746, I will think of you, give thanks for you, and pray you come to understand just how much God loves you."

And so I have. We've even managed to keep in contact via e-mail a time or two. Each time her name appears in my inbox, I give thanks to God. After all, he uniquely fit together all the details—the "small things" —in both our lives so that we could meet.

Yes, the small things.

The details we so easily miss . . . or discount . . . because they don't seem important. And yet the God who created the universe is also the God of the small things.

For instance, because he is omniscient, all-knowing, he knew, in advance, that Renata and I would meet. What exactly was it that drew me to Renata—even more than her startling green eyes? It was God himself, drawing my soul to another hopeful soul. A soul who was longing for the "small things" in her life to make sense. Who was longing for the "something more" all of us long for.

For, you see, all of us have the hope of the eternal woven into our hearts—God himself made sure of it.[3] And I will never forget him using me to be a "small" part of increasing one woman's faith, sustaining her hope, and compelling her to grasp the Love which is eternal.

✷ ✷ ✷

How important it is, in the light of hope, to see God in the "small things" of life!

What do I mean by "small things"? Small things are those tiny details, those tiny reminders that provide encouragement and hope, just when we need it. The small things that are sometimes such an integral part of our life that we tend to forget about them.

What small things have made an impact on me?

SMALL THING #1: PERSONAL CORRESPONDENCE

I have stashed within file cabinets, storage boxes, plastic totes, and innumerable office paper boxes nearly every card, letter, and note I have ever received. And every one has touched my life in a special way when I got it. There is a note card with these words: "If you're not going to SNORT, why even laugh?" Sent from my traveling buddy, Becky, it arrived on a day when I had very little to laugh about. How did she and God know it would be a small thing at just the right time?

Three weeks before the extended deadline for this book (*I'd already missed the first deadline*) and six minutes before I thought my head was going to blow up, a card arrived in my mailbox from a meeting planner I would be working with in the near future. In it was a card with the following message: "This is God calling. I'll be taking care of everything from here on out. Relax."

I love it! Small, timely, *and* funny.

Hanging on the wall above my computer is a 3 x 2 corkboard. Pinned to the board is a birthday card with a very kind personal note from my friend Anne, as well as one from my mother. My mother's cards always mean a lot because she takes lots and lots of time picking them out. She's determined they will say just the right words. *(Sigh: I, on the other hand, go to the card section, look for the overall topic I need and just pluck and pay for the first one I grab. Shame on me . . .).*

Secured next to them is a Christmas ornament my youngest child made when he was in second grade, as well as three or four e-mails I printed and posted based on their encouraging or oddball message. *(And speaking of oddball—run to your nearest Barnes & Noble and purchase a box of Zelda cards. They are hilarious and have just the kind of quirky humor that is guaranteed to perk up the spirit of its intended recipient.)*

SMALL THING #2: COMFORT FOOD

Now honestly, what kind of food do you want to sit down to when you're in need of a little assurance and rest? Are you going to grab for the chilled celery sticks? Or the 19-grain bread slice that weighs more than your firstborn did at birth? When you walk into your mother's home or show up for dinner at the home of a close friend, do you want them encouraging your spirit with the aroma of simmering, low-cal beets?

I think not!

And dare you think I'm advocating a diet loaded with carbs, starch, sugar, and fat, let me be the first to say, "I am."

Maybe not for the long haul—or even four days out of the week—but everyone needs to experience, at some point or another, the "small thing" rightness of a roast-beef dinner with sides of mashed potatoes, macaroni and cheese, garden-fresh sweet corn slathered in butter, and homemade yeast rolls . . . all followed with a chaser of rich, dark gravy. Hmm . . . anybody else hungry?

And let's just say it, girls: There is nothing like chocolate to lift the mood. And the sugar-free variety or the imitation carob chocolate simply doesn't cut it. So why not go for the "small thing" of the real deal and treat yourself every once in a while?

I don't think I'm going too far when I say Jesus himself recognized the "small thing" importance of meals spent together. Consider the time spent at the home of his dear friends Mary, Martha, and Lazarus. I can only imagine there was quite a feast of hope and rejoicing after one particular time Jesus came to see them![4] And don't forget it was over a meal in which he spent his last moments with all 12 of his disciples and then another, only days later, when the 11 who remained saw with their eyes the wounds of The One they loved.[5]

So what do you think? You want to come over for a little something to eat?

SMALL THING #3: MUSIC

They say music can tame the savage beast, but I can tell you from personal experience that it has the power to tame a restless and hopeless heart too.

The very first time I can recall this occurring was when I was about seven years old. I had received a record player *(okay, so now I've dated myself again)* for Christmas, and my mom had purchased *(as she would say)* "a whole slew" of records. I had Alvin and the Chipmunks, a red plastic album (not to be confused with *The White Album*) that I seldom played but always thought looked really cool, and a set of Walt Disney musical sound tracks—my favorite being *Mary Poppins*.

My mother probably thought she was going to lose her mind after hearing "Feed the Birds" for the millionth time. But oh, how I loved that song! Whenever I felt sad, I could just place my stereophonic needle on the spinning disk, listen to the rather melancholy melody line and lyrics, and immediately I felt better! It was like someone understood me after all.

In eighth grade I ordered a K-Tel record, *Get Up and Boogie*, and waited approximately nine months for it to arrive. By the time it landed in the oversize-package area of Postmaster Bob Greenfield's mail room, disco was dead *(And that's probably for the best, as I'm not sure "Love to Love You Baby" qualifies as an appropriate example.)*

Moving on . . . in 1981 I heard a song by contemporary Christian artist Keith Green. At the time I felt like the sorriest excuse for a Christian ever. I wasn't doing anything right and doing everything wrong. I said I believed one thing, then I'd turn around and do something that disproved it. I had lost all hope of ever doing things right, and I was only 15 years old. Then I heard one of Keith's songs. It was the right song at the right time, and its lyrics allowed me to believe again. The song? "Grace by Which I Stand." It was a small thing, but God knew—

right at that moment—I needed to hear that music. And that
the words would again give courage, belief, and hope to my
hurting heart.

My mind also returns to an evening spent waiting next to the
crib of my then eight-week-old son, who had been hospitalized
for breathing complications. As I watched him struggle to inhale,
then exhale, I found my lips returning to a song from childhood:

> *My hope is built on nothing less*
> *Than Jesus' blood and righteousness;*
> *I dare not trust the sweetest frame,*
> *But wholly lean on Jesus' name.*
> *On Christ the solid rock I stand;*
> *All other ground is sinking sand.*[6]

Sweet counsel and sweet truth is what I found in those wonderful old lyrics.

Girlfriend, think back to the times God has used music to reach
your heart. Think of the times he has spoken through lyrics of
songs, both contemporary and hymns of old, and has given *you*
a reason to hope. Why not make a list for yourself in a journal or
on a piece of paper and listen to those songs again?

✳ ✳ ✳

Let us never discount the holiness of small things—musical or
otherwise.

For God, not the devil, has been in the details since before
time began.

In the beginning he spoke four small words, "Let there be light," and the sun warmed the earth.[7]

On a late afternoon Jesus fed five thousand men, women, and children with five loaves and two fish given by a child.[8]

He also told us that faith the size of a mustard seed *(very, very small)* can produce results beyond imagination.[9]

And he promised each and every one of us reading these pages that the life we live now, which may seem filled with all manner of smallness and insignificance, is being used for purposes of eternal value.

On earth and in the one to come.

✳ 6 ✳

This I Know to Be True

"It's Gore-Tex . . . you know about Gore-Tex?"[1]

Ah, yes. George Costanza, the quirky little *Seinfeld* character, and I know a thing or two about Gore-Tex!

You see, every day in winter, after layering my body with chenille socks, two sets of flannel lounge pants, and a fleece hoodie, I slip my arms through said Michelin Man-inspired outerwear. Quickly zipping and snapping the front secure, I then balance myself from left to right foot as I shove my feet into what can only be described as a pair of "criminally ugly" boots. No self-respecting woman under the age of 35 would ever be caught wearing these. I'm 39, so there you go.

Next I pull a pair of fully lined and insulated mittens on, toss a hand-knitted mohair scarf dramatically around my face and neck, and attempt to grab a stained SpongeBob stocking cap *(one of my children's, of course, not mine. I do have some shred of dignity left . . .)* from a jumbled basket of said objects.

It takes a couple of minutes, especially since I've got mittens the size of small turkeys to work with. When at last SpongeBob sits securely on my head, I do a quick cross-check of zippers and snaps. Against my better judgment I steal a glance into the nearby bathroom mirror.

Yep, it's official. I have the exact rotund proportions of that "blueberry" girl in the movie *Willie Wonka and the Chocolate Factory.*

Nice. *Real* nice.

I then snap a pair of plate-size earmuffs on as I open the back door and waddle 20 feet to a frozen metal box, where I attempt to retrieve my mail *(picture my mittens as a set of salad tongs grabbing at the envelopes)* on yet another bitterly cold winter day in Western Illinois.

✳ ✳ ✳

I've heard it said, quite often in fact, that man can live 40 days without food, three days without water, and not one second without hope. Well, I'd like to rephrase that, if you don't mind.

Woman *(i.e., me)* can live 40 days without food, three days without water, and not one second without the hope of summer.

You think I'm kidding? Let me assure you, I am not. *(I mentioned earlier that my favorite place in the world is a beach, didn't I? And how much I love warm, sunny weather?)*

Winter has to be one of the loneliest and most "where is the hope"-inducing times of the year for me. Maybe it's the overall grayness accompanying winter in Illinois that brings my spirits down and my weight up. *(That or the 14 pounds of Exquisite Fudge—this tantalizing recipe is included on page 155—that I consume while being held hostage in my home by chill factors and razor-sharp winds.)* Maybe it has something to do with the sun not shining for nearly five months. Or maybe it's the frozen car locks or the cold that seeps through exterior walls, insulation, and draperies to settle into your house and your bones.

Or maybe it's all of the above things and a million more!

✳ ✳ ✳

Life has a way of chipping away at the things we know are true and slowly diminishing hope within us. I have felt it, and so have myriad women I've talked with over the years. So if you find yourself in the same camp, you're in good company *(and surrounded with a lot of empathy too).*

Surprisingly, I find it's not so much us *choosing* to declare we're officially giving up hope as it is us awaking one morning and realizing that hope has somehow slipped from our grasp. That all the things of life have accumulated into a heavy weariness of soul so we cannot even lift our heads to see what might be ahead.

Have you ever found yourself *there,* my friend? Realizing that you have

✳ no hope for today, tomorrow, or anything in the future
✳ no hope of heaven
✳ no hope for laughter
✳ no hope for love
✳ no hope for new beginnings
✳ no hope for second chances
✳ no hope for grace

✳ no hope for forgiveness

✳ no hope . . . for even hope itself.

In other words, you're completely wrung dry of hope. If that's you, then I beg you: Hold on for just a bit longer. Don't give up. And don't believe the whispering lie of the devil that you're alone in this. You are far from that, my friend. In fact, I'm right beside you. Here—scoot that beach towel of yours a little closer, and let me get you a drink refill. . . .

✳ ✳ ✳

Truth is, each winter I am faced with the same weight of hope-lessness *(in fact, I've recently read some articles about SAD—Seasonal Affective Disorder—and have wondered if they are talking about me).* And each winter I am confronted with the same choice: Should I leave my family, or take them with me to Bermuda? *(I'm kidding, of course, but in my lowest-of-low times I have seriously considered it.)*

So, knowing the thoughts and emotions I'll have for five months of the year, *every year,* what can I do?

WHAT IS HOPE, REALLY?

I think it all comes down to my definition of hope. What is hope, really?

Through my seasons of "wallowing in winter," I've come to believe that hope is a soul's response to the promises of God. Promises that tell us

✳ who our hope is anchored to

and

✳ what our response to life is, based on the truths God plants within us when we trust him.

"Hope is our fuel for the journey," writes author and scholar Lewis Smedes. "As long as we keep hope alive, we keep moving. To stop moving is to die of hope deficiency."[2]

A 17th-century author, William Gurnall, wrote with a heart tuned to the 21st-century when he noted:

When a hound has lost the scent, he hunts backward to recover it and pursues his game with a louder cry of confidence than before. Thus, Christian, when your hope is at a loss and you question your salvation in another world, look backward to see what God has done for you in this one. . . . Past experiences with God are a sure foundation for hope in future hardships and also a powerful argument in prayer . . . . So you should not only feast with the joy of mercy, but have the remembrance of it as hope-seed, to strengthen you to wait on God for further mercy and help in time of need.[3]

Could you use some fuel for your journey through life? I sure could!

So where can we find this fuel? Read on!

PLANTING THE SEEDS OF HOPE

During the dark of winter, seeds and bulbs rest in the cold soil, waiting for the fuel of spring's moisture and the stroke of the sun to warm them before they push through the chill and into the sunshine. And when they sprout, they make a beautiful spring-time harvest!

When you are facing a spiritually brutal cold spell, it's important to remember that although the seeds of truth may seem "dead," they are still alive. And they are still guaranteed to bring a harvest of hope when you and those around you need it most.

What seeds of truth am I talking about?

Seed of Truth #1: God will show up.

I alluded to the "unchangeable" promises of God as found in his divinity and nature in an earlier chapter. This time I'd like you to read for yourself God's spoken and revealed promises—promises that God made long before time ever began. Even before you were a "gleam" in your mother's eye!

In fact, we'll start right in Jeremiah 29:10-11, where God promises to always be by our side:

"I'll show up and take care of you as I promised and bring you back home. I know what I'm doing. I have it all planned out—plans to take care of you, not abandon you, plans to give you the future you hope for."[4]

Do you recall reading this verse earlier in the book? You did, indeed, as part of the incredible truth of God being unable to lie. I want to remind you of that as you read this promise and the ones that are to follow.

But here's my caveat: *Do not* just skim these, thinking, *Yada, yada, yeah, right. I've heard these before. Read them before.* Please, don't do that! Take the time to slow down and to truly think through each phrase of that verse. Truth is, God has his eye on *you*. Wow! Not only that, but he is *actively* working in your life through the people, experiences, difficulties, and successes to bring about the ultimate hope of eternal life found when you live your life for him.

I absolutely love the promise of his presence in chapter 40 (verses 27 through 31) of the Old Testament book of Isaiah:

> *"Why would you ever complain, O Jacob,*
> *or whine, Israel, saying,*
> *'God has lost track of me.*
> *He doesn't care what happens to me'?*
> *Don't you know anything? Haven't you been listening?*
> *God doesn't come and go. God lasts.*
> *He's Creator of all you can see or imagine.*
> *He doesn't get tired out, doesn't pause to catch his breath.*
> *And he knows everything, inside and out.*
> *He energizes those who get tired, gives fresh strength to*
> *dropouts.*
> *For even young people tire and drop out,*
> *young folk in their prime stumble and fall.*
> *But those who wait upon God get fresh strength.*
> *They spread their wings and soar like eagles,*
> *They run and don't get tired,*
> *they walk and don't lag behind."*[5]

Am I the only woman who feels like she could run a marathon after reading those truths?

I memorized this portion of the Bible as a junior in college *(January 6, 1986, as I noted in the page margin of my Bible)* and every time I read it now, I still feel like that 19-year-old woman who wanted nothing more than to please God and to love him.

In fact, while I was typing those words just now, I read them aloud. And I was reminded of his faithfulness in my life.

I thought of the hundreds of prayers he has heard and answered.

I thought of the comfort he has provided through other women when the prayers answered *(or those I thought had gone unanswered)* were hard to understand and difficult to accept.

I thought of how many times I have grown tired and have whined my way through a week, a month . . . oh, all right, you got me! Through an *entire* season!

And I heard again in my heart, that faint whisper: *God* lasts, *Julie, God* lasts.

Dear one, God can't lie, and he can't go against a promise he has made toward us—toward you.

God told the Israelites, "I've never quit loving you and never will. Expect love, love, and more love!"[6]

Unlike humans, perhaps, who have disappointed you in the past with unkept promises, God *will* always show up. It's an unchangeable part of his nature.

Will you plant this seed of truth and allow God to nurture and water it within you? Will you trust God to grow the sprout of hope where there is distrust? I promise you will not be disappointed!

Seed of Truth #2: The past gives confidence.
The only way we can look forward with confidence and hope is if we can look back with confidence and hope. This is why I urge women to invest in some form of journaling. It can be as simple

as writing down quick notes in a Bible or filling pages of a note-book with thoughts and remembrances.

It doesn't matter where you write. Just write.

Keep notes of prayers asked and answered. Be specific and note the month, day, and year *(I always put them in parentheses, after my request)*. Here are some real-life samples, taken from the pages and margins of my Bible, which have fueled my own hope in God.

✳ Bring home the kidnapped hostages in Iran safely. (April 1986)

✳ Performed a monologue (The Ragman) for the retired teachers in Brunswick. They really seemed to listen. God, I don't know if all the people there understand what it means to believe in you. But you do. Please take all that happened and use it so they might believe in you. (November 14, 1986)

✳ God, gave Rick a promotion at work, and with his increase in pay, I can now stay home with the baby!!! (May 17, 1988)

✳ Learned I was pregnant with baby #2! We are so happy. (August 31, 1989)

✳ John McCarthy, former hostage, released. (August 24, 1990)

✳ Lord, you know the limbo Rick and I are in right now. I pray that your will be done in his move to another division at work. You know we both want to stay close to our families. But we also want you to send us where you know is best. God, we're going to trust you completely on this. You've never let us down before. (July 14, 1991)

✳ Alan Steen, former hostage, released. (August 13, 1991)

✳ Jerry Anderson, FINAL former hostage, released.
(December 4, 1991)

✳ Misty White came home after one year of hospitalization!
Our church has been praying for her all this time. Thank
you, God. (December 1991)

✳ Found out a good friend of Rick's is dying from cancer.
Please heal him. (September 1992)

✳ Rick's friend died—I don't understand why you allowed this
to happen. He was only 22 years old. What's the point in
taking him when he was so talented and loved you so much?
I don't understand, but I choose to trust in you.
(April 19, 1993)

Each time I come across the above writings, remember the
agony and then the answer to prayer on the date noted, or find
a specific Bible verse with an arrow and comment pointing to it,
a hope-seed is planted and begins to take root. As the sprout
grows, so does my faith in God.

What about you? Is there a journal or perhaps a Bible with
scribbled notes that you can turn to in order to be reminded of
God's specific promises kept and your prayers answered? If not,
why not start one today?

Treat yourself to a nice journal—one with pages that turn
easily and provide ample space for writing. Or maybe you need
a new Bible. I'll let you in on a little secret: I choose my Bibles
on two criteria.

1. That it's a sound translation of the original language
   of the Old and New Testaments.

2. That there are lots and lots of white pages and wide margins just waiting to be filled with remembrances and thanks.

So don't wait any longer, girls. Put this book down right now and head out the door to buy one. You'll be glad you did!

How else do I actively "remember the past"? I remember the "summer" times of my life.

Crazy as it may seem, I keep a bottle of Coppertone sun-tanning lotion on my desk area, as well as in our downstairs bathroom cabinet. Every now and then, in the middle of winter, when I'm starting to contemplate a one-way ticket to Fiji, I pull out that bottle, push down on the pour lid, gently squeeze its sides, and take a long, coconut-scented hit. Ah, yes, the aroma of summer!

And since I spend a large portion of my time writing in my basement office, I have taken to stapling sheets of ocean blue paper on the wall directly in front of me. This is what I stare at when my brain is fried, when my fingers are tingling from overuse of the computer keyboard, and I'm suffering overall from poor creative productivity. This is what I stare at when the darker side of my mind whispers to my heart, *Why don't you just give up this writing thing? You're really not all that good at it, anyway.*

I look at those papers with the color of summer skies and ocean depths, and the view calms me—it restores my hope in a crazy, stapled-to-the-wall kind of way.

I also pull out photographs and postcards from favorite summer activities, like our family vacation to the Lake of the Ozarks.

I ask the kids questions at the dinner table, such as, "What is your favorite memory of our time spent at Cedar Point Resort and its fabulous water park?" *(Even if I do get the famous eye-rolls at this "Let's Make Mom Feel Better" trip through Memory Lane, the experience does make me feel better!)*

Girlfriend, what favorite memories of times "in the sun"— whether physical or emotional—do you recall? Why not snuggle up in a favorite place and take a few minutes to jot down your specific memories of that time *(in that new journal or Bible you just purchased, of course)*. Journal about *why* that time was so special to you. It will bring a smile now, as you relive the memories, and you can also reread that journal entry later, when "winter" creeps upon your soul again.

Seed of Truth #3: You can look ahead with anticipation.
As each cold, dreary day passes into the next cold day and the next dreary week of winter, I look ahead with anticipation.

What do I mean by that?

Five years ago I planted over 300 bulbs around a brick pathway and in varying places in our yard. I told my husband that I'd be able to manage the winter somehow if I could look forward to a spring and summertime filled with the vibrant colors of crocuses, daffodils, tulips, snowdrops, and lilies.

In a sense, I planted hope. The hope of new life. The product of sun and warmth.

So now, when I'm cloaked in Gore-Tex in the winter, I think of brilliant, yellow daffodils that will soon line the sidewalk.

When I'm hammering out paragraphs and wondering if they make any sense whatsoever, I think of four dozen purple crocuses that will break free from the cold earth and brighten the vine-covered dirt in front of my office window.

And when I feel my spirits drooping, I think of the emerging bright green of new grass that is easing its way upward out of the cold soil. I envision all the other lovely red, white, purple, pink, orange, and blue flowers that will explode in a wild proliferation of joy all over my yard, come spring.

When I can't find hope, hope has an exquisite way of finding me . . . through the promises of what will be.

What makes *you* want to look ahead—to the promises of what will be?

Why not start by filling the pages of that journal or Bible you just bought sometime before you head for bed tonight?

Seed of Truth #4: Jesus is our Hope.[7]

Now to our fourth and final seed of truth—hope is a noun. It's all about Jesus.

Remember that hymn I thought of while watching over my sick eight-week-old baby? The words that came to mind time and time again acted as a balm of healing to my scared and nervous soul:

> *My hope is built on nothing less*
> *than Jesus' blood and righteousness. . . .*[8]

We have a wonderful family physician, Dr. Keith Peachey, and I knew the staff of Cottage Medical Hospital was doing its best to help my son, Patrick. But when it came down to the brass tacks of hope and trust, ladies, it was the name of Jesus and the history

I had with him that gave me hope to believe things would be all right. That no matter what happened, my sweet little boy was safe in the arms of Jesus. Safe in the arms of our ultimate Hope. And when I write the words *all right,* I mean hope to believe that even if little Patrick didn't make it, things would be all right. For Patrick. And for me.

Whew. I could never pray, believe, or think that way except for my solid faith in Jesus—yes, even in the midst of shaky times—and my hope that God is, at his core, good and kind. And that he has, at his very heart, my best interests in mind.

To answer a question posed in the first chapter: I don't believe faith, hope, and love can be separated.

They are a three-strand cord of virtue that draws us closer to the heart of God.

Without faith it is impossible to please God.[9]

By faith we believe in Christ.

Our hope in Christ makes us unashamed.

And love is the greatest of them all.[10]

7

Are We There Yet?

One of the longest trips of my life took place about three years ago.

In the confines of our 1994 Ford Windstar minivan were the following: our three children, two coolers filled with drinks and snacks, four 12-packs of Pepsi, four suitcases, five winter coats (in case we had car trouble in a cold state), a bag of water shoes *(make that slightly mildewed water shoes)* from a trip to somewhere warm and sunny three years previous, two book bags crammed with homework to be finished over the holiday break, three sets of headphones with eight-foot cords, and a portable television with DVD player *(but without DVDs. In our flurry, Rick and I had somehow forgotten them).*

Due to these circumstances *(some within our control, had we organized ourselves a little better),* we found ourselves utterly and completely abandoning a previously held parental ban against a certain animated cartoon family.

Think about it, ladies.

My husband and I would be traveling with our three children

in the minivan with nothing to entertain them for the next 18 hours of our lives. *(You're feeling my pain, aren't you?)*

I make no apologies for what happened next.

Who among you can say you wouldn't have cracked under the same pressure?

Let those of you who have never ridden in a van with three siblings annoying one another, breathing on one another, or touching one another cast the first digital video disc as a stone.

We were desperate, I tell you. *Desperate.*

So I found myself entering through the electronic gates of Stuff-Mart heaven. Bypassing a book rack to my left *(after quickly checking to see if any of my titles were on it. Drat!)* and zipping past the well-zoned areas of chocolate M&M's and cheap generic Ho Hos, I headed like a crazed woman to the electronics section.

I didn't have much time.

I had left Rick in the van with all three inmates . . . er, *children* . . . and I knew from previous history that there would be three, maybe four minutes tops, before his eyes would begin to roll to the top of his head and he'd begin stammering out threats like, "If you guys don't stop it right now, your mother and I will just leave you right here, call your grandparents and tell them to pick you up, and go on to Disney World all by ourselves!"

They would, of course, laugh.

He would, of course, wish he'd never agreed to drive all the way to Florida.

So there I was, standing in the movie section with my husband's life hanging in the balance. *Quick, quick,* I told myself, *just pick a good movie and get out of here.* I picked up one, read the back, and placed it back. *Hmm, guess I'll have to go straight to the family section.* So I go to that section and stare for 45 seconds or so and realize there is nothing that fits the likes of a 7-, 12-, and 13-year-old all in one shot.

The seconds were ticking fast.

I could imagine Rick clearing his throat and sticking his head out of the window for air as I stood there.

Hurry, hurry, hurry! Just buy something that'll keep them happy to Memphis.

Then I spied it.

It was on sale and included six DVD discs. Yes, six discs! That would be enough to carry them speechless to Jacksonville—and, with a little luck, all the way to Orlando.

So I paid for that little greatest hits box, headed straight for the white minivan with the drooping back end *(an amazing metaphor for my life),* handed over the first of six discs to Kristen *(the de-facto leader of the three)* and said, "Here, watch this while I attempt to give your dad CPR."

Rick was revived.

The disc was inserted.

Headphones were placed over ears.

And all was right with the world for approximately 42 minutes. That's when we heard a particular gust of laughter from the kids. Then Ricky Neal shouted over the television volume being pumped into his eardrums, "Mom! I can't believe you finally bought us *The Simpsons!*" as his brother and sister picked up the mantra being chanted on screen by one Bart Simpson: "Are we there yet, are we there yet, are we there yet, are we there yet, are we . . ."

Doh! I should have picked a disc set highlighting silent movies from the 1920s.

✳ ✳ ✳

Do you remember those unbearably long car trips from your youth?

Perhaps you were headed to a favorite relative's house, like me. I can remember going to my aunt Joanie's house in Keytesville, Missouri. She was my mom's twin sister, and she made the best ham-and-mayo sandwiches I had ever tasted. Every Saturday or Sunday afternoon my mom and I *(sometimes my dad if he hadn't already fallen asleep in his recliner watching Sunday football)* would drive over to visit with her and my uncle Gene.

For me as an eight-year-old, Keytesville may as well have been 1,200 miles from my hometown of Brunswick, for as long as it seemed to take to get there. But I'd keep my eyes peeled for the markers I had come to recognize along the way. First we passed Jr.'s West End Grocery *(the same Junior who always sent me home with a Chocolate Soldier pop),* then came Moser's Coffee Shop, King Hill, Melba Shipp's house, and the Dalton Junction.

Were we there yet?

Not by a long shot.

So as my mother drove along, I kept my hope fixed on pecan farms, soybean fields, and the low-laying bottoms that were periodically flooded out by the creek that flows underneath the Keytesville city bridge and population sign. I watched and I counted each one as yet another sure sign that we were almost there.

At last, as our car drove past the county courthouse, the statue of General Sterling Price, and Prengers' IGA, I would hear the familiar click of mom's turn signal. Our car would turn left on Ash Street. It was then just a bit past the car wash where we would turn right into the driveway of Aunt Joanie's.

Well, it was about time! *(13 minutes from start to finish . . .)*

Then, before my mother had even turned off the car's engine, I would go running into the house, just drooling in anticipation. I knew a wonderful treat would await me—a sandwich of white bread *(crusts removed with razor sharp knife)* with thin ham slices covered with Miracle Whip *(my mom was committed to Hellmann's)*.

As I would take the very first bite, my eyes would close in delight.

Yum! That sandwich was worth every minute I'd spent looking forward to it too. Somehow the taste in my mouth always surpassed what I had even expected.

And just one bite would wipe away all the long minutes of "Are we there yet?"

✳ ✳ ✳

Are we there yet? It's the periodic question and complaint of children *(and adults)* when they find themselves tired of sitting still and seemingly getting nowhere when heading toward a highly anticipated destination.

Are we there yet? acknowledges *this*—the place where we are,

right now—isn't all there is. There is something greater, something more fulfilling, something our souls can do nothing about
but desire.

Are we there yet? speaks to the heart longing to find rest
amidst a day full of interruptions, letdowns, and worries.

Are we there yet? points our gaze, yet again, to The One able
to provide refuge, safe harbor, and sanctuary—on our way to
work as well as on our journey through life to heaven.

The truth is, if we're moving in the direction of our destination, then we're never truly sitting still, no matter how slow our
process may seem. Every mile marker we pass *(be it hometown
landmark or interstate billboard)* is simply one more sighting
reminding us of where we are and where we're ultimately
heading.

In the next few pages I'd like you to consider a few of the
mile markers I believe God has given us all as encouragement
along the road to heaven. And I want to share with you a few
specific people, places, and events that have dotted the land-
scape of my faith, both past and present, with the tantalizing
promise that hope is on the way.

MILE MARKER #1: PSALM 62:5-8

> *"God, the one and only—*
> *I'll wait as long as he says.*
> *Everything I hope for comes from him,*
> *so why not?*
> *He's solid rock under my feet,*
> *breathing room for my soul,*
> *An impregnable castle:*

I'm set for life.
My help and glory are in God
--granite-strength and safe-harbor-God --
So trust him absolutely, people;
lay your lives on the line for him.
God is a safe place to be."[1]

I'd like to confess something while we're lying here on the beach, if you don't mind. It may not seem like all that big a deal to you when you read it, but it's been bugging me for some time now. And after reading the preceding verses, well, I'd like to just say it. Maybe seeing it in print for thousands to see and read will help me do something about it.

Okay, here it is. . . . I am addicted to news and information.

Now, let me explain why I think this may not be such a good thing.

You see, every morning when I wake up, the first thing I tend to grab is . . . *not* my Bible. *(Nor is it my husband, for he's usually left for work a good 30 minutes before I drag myself out from under the covers.)* No, I'm usually grabbing a television remote control so I can tune in to the *FOX & Friends* morning news show.

Or, if I can't find the remote control to the television I swore 18 years ago would never be in my bedroom, I make my way downstairs to my office *(i.e., our basement)* and mouse and click my way to www.drudgereport.com, where I read the latest tragedy, scandal, threat, or similarly uplifting news item, before I even greet my children good morning.

Or even before I say hello to God, for that matter.

Herein lies the problem with my addiction, ladies.

I take my bad news hit and guess what I feel?

You got it! I feel hope *less.*

But when I read the divine words encouraging me to wait for God and to let him be the solid rock under my feet, I feel *hope full.* And I think, *Sign me up!* How well I know that I need a solid foundation in all the shaky places of my life and in our uncertain world.

I read and say aloud the words, "God is a safe place to be," and I feel safe. I desire to rest in the security of him in all ways.

I have such *good* intentions . . . and, sadly, such weak follow-through.

I think of all the mornings *(as well as afternoons and evenings)* when I never think of God or the security he offers because my mind is stuck in the rut of reading about and/or listening to potential terror threats and economic worries.

But it shouldn't be like this, I know.

I shouldn't be like this.

I know that my trust and my hope can be found in God alone. So why is it such a temptation for me to entrench myself in the "news of the day"? Perhaps it's my innate "snoopiness"—the voyeuristic, "inquiring mind wants to know" part of me. For who of us doesn't want to be "in the know," ladies? Yet some, like myself, take it to the extreme.

However, reading Psalm 62 is a solemn reminder for me. No matter how many breaking news stories I may read or how much information I may gather about any number of inane subjects, God is my safe place. And the only way I'm going to learn to trust and hope in him is by spending less time in the news and more time with The One who offers Good News.[2]

MILE MARKER #2: ROMANS 5:1-5

"Therefore, since we have been justified through faith, we have peace with God through our Lord Jesus Christ, through whom we have gained access by faith into this grace in which we now stand. And we rejoice in the hope of the glory of God. Not only so, but we also rejoice in our sufferings, because we know that suffering produces persever-ance; perseverance, character; and character, hope. And hope does not disappoint us, because God has poured out his love into our hearts by the Holy Spirit, whom he has given us."[3] (Romans 5:1-5, NIV)

I like the way the last portion of this hopeful truth is translated in *The Message:* "In alert expectancy [hope] such as this, we're never left feeling shortchanged."[4]

Interesting word usage when you think about it: *shortchanged.* To feel *shortchanged* is to feel cheated, to feel as though you are getting less than what is justly expected. But why on earth would any of us feel cheated, as it were, by God? And if we indeed felt that very thing—as though we were prom-ised or "sold" a cheap imitation of hope that failed to deliver during the hard times and the dark times—what is to become of us? What is to become of hope and God?

Hmm, I have dabbled more than a bit in this pot of emo-tional and spiritual angst. For there have been plenty of times when I've felt frustrated, yes, shortchanged when it comes to certain matters with God. I've wondered on more than one occasion what he was doing (or thinking) regarding some area of my life. Or perhaps, more typically, what I've thought he *should* be doing about a problem in another person's life. And yes, sometimes the "problem" I see that needs to be fixed is that particular individual's entire makeup—i.e., personality, attitude, temperament, and/or mere existence. *(Hmm, why is it so much easier to want to change someone else before we change ourselves? Perhaps it has something to do with our need for more grace and more forgiveness?)*

But more often than not, my mounting frustration has come as a result of watching friends and family I care deeply about ask for God's help (and I'm talking "only God can help in this situation" type prayer) or intervention, only to see it not happen. Or at least not happen in a tangible manner that quells my immediate need for their problem to be fixed or removed or diminished.

From that comes the feeling of being shortchanged—of not getting the prayer goods delivered as I believed they should or would be. I confess, ladies, there have been times when I've felt as though a cosmic switch-and-bait ruse occurred before my very eyes, despite my head screaming, *You know this isn't true, Julie!*

And then I felt really, really, *really* crummy, crass, and pretty much useless as a Christian for even thinking such a thing.

Anyone else out there empathize with the pathetic creature I sometimes am?

This is why the hope-that-does-not-disappoint mile marker is so important. For often I find myself, at best, plodding along, dazed and confused. I desperately need to know there is truth on which to plant my feet—right here, right now.

Not surprisingly, I have, at times, questioned my own love for God. And I suppose a portion of that questioning is a result of my own expectation that by age 39 I would somehow have a firmer grasp on such matters of faith—and hope.

I expected, by age 39, to have a broader understanding of the "deep" things of God.

Here I am, 39 years old, and I don't even know what the deep things are.

I expected to be able to quote Bible verses, chapter and verse, from Genesis to Revelation and even throw in a few Holy Land geographical points just to show off.

Here I am, 39 years old, and I'm lucky if I can quote you my newest cell phone number—or pinpoint its specific geographical position in my home.

I expected to be a woman of immeasurable faith, limitless mercy, and one even willing to wash a few feet to show just how humble and hospitable she was.

Here I am, 39 years old, and my faith could fit in a thimble. I scored a zero on a test that evaluated one's natural proclivity for being merciful, and the only feet I've been anxious to wash *(all right, the only feet I've been* willing *to wash)* are the ones squarely attached to my own puffy ankles.

Sigh.

I must admit, in many ways I have turned out to be quite a disappointment to myself, and sometimes I have even been disappointed with God.

Yes, I wrote and you read, "I have been disappointed with God."

Now here's how my skewed thinking works in regards to such matters. I believe God is in control of everything, yet he allows *(even delights)* in giving us the freedom to choose to love him, obey him, serve him, and even wash one another's feet as a symbol of service. I also believe God has plans and dreams for our lives,[5] and he takes great pleasure in seeing those plans fulfilled. Furthermore, I believe God is good, kind, and just, and desires good things for every human who has lived, will ever live, and is living now.

I believe these things, yet I find myself in the middle of life—praying for women whose cancer has metastasized to their liver or brain; women whose children have been admitted to psych wards; women who have begged their husbands to get help for their pornography addiction; women who can't seem to break free from their own addictions with pornography, alcohol, or any number of shameful secrets. I believe, yet I watch with horror as 10-year-olds are reported abducted, abused, and then murdered, on my local news at 10. I have no answers *(and my own faith diminishes)* as 200,000 people are swept away in a tsunami of end-times proportion. I live in the same place you do, in the midst of evil, suffering, pain, and unexplained death. And, despite my strongest attempts against it, I find myself disappointed with God.

I believe God is in control of everything.

I believe God allows us the freedom to choose to love, obey, follow, and behave like decent human beings.

I believe God has plans for everyone ever created and born.

I believe God is good, just, and kind.

But I am oftentimes conflicted as to how he works. And why he works the way he does.

How about you? Has hope in God ever disappointed you?

It's okay to say, "Yes," if that's the way you feel. Remember, we're sitting here, girlfriend to girlfriend, on our beach blankets in the warm sun and sharing our hearts. Any secret you have is safe with me. *(Let's just say you've certainly heard a lot of mine.)*

Truth is, each of us has had a different experience with God.

Some of you reading the pages of *Exquisite Hope* find believing in God and trusting in hope to be as easy and comfortable as slipping on a pair of house slippers. *(Neon green Steve Madden's perhaps?)* Even in rough times, your faith does not waiver.

But others of you have had to scratch and scrap for even a shred of trust. Maybe you're like my friend Annie, who learned early in life, through horrific childhood experiences, that she could trust no one. That fear of trusting anyone other than herself has carried over to her experience of trusting God.

Others of you need to discover the lavish riches of scandalous grace before you can even believe God would desire to know you. *(And oh, how he longs for you to know him!)*

Others of you need to cling to the radical nature of forgiveness if you are ever to find peace from your past.

And others of you will have to wrestle with troubles and patience and integrity before you feel you can say for yourself: "God is a safe place to be."

How well God knows us! And that's why he gives us mile markers, all throughout Scripture, for the journey home. Mile markers like Romans 5:1-5 so that we might know what is true, trust what is good, and think on them all.

You see, in the midst of my handwringing and spiritual navel gazing, I am gently reminded of our mile marker: "Hope does not disappoint us because God has poured out his love into our hearts by the Holy Spirit, whom he has given us."

It all comes down to the fact that I expected to be a bit further down the road in certain matters. I certainly have been disappointed in my own inability to hold fast to what he says he will and can do. Yet I know, in and through all these things, he has been pouring out his love into my heart. *(Remember the picture of lavish grace being poured out into our lives? So, too, it is with God's love and hope!)* This hope is an anchor, for I will surely continue to disappoint myself and God as the years go by. But God will never leave me, give up on me, or feel shortchanged in my creation.

MILE MARKER #3: ROMANS 15:4

"For whatever was written in earlier times was written for our instruction, so that through perseverance and the encouragement of the Scriptures we might have hope."[6]

You know about that little allergy thing I have regarding shellfish, right? Well, there's something else that triggers swelling and itching. I try to avoid it as pointedly as I do shrimp.

"It" would be the title of "Expert."

Ugh. I nearly pass out when producers and interviewers refer to me as "an *expert* on anger and motherhood," "an *expert* on finances" *(clearly they had not read* 'Til Debt Do Us Part *in its entirety)*, or "an *expert* on the spiritual life."

Ack! You can almost watch the hive patches appear instantly.

And while I understand the semantics of introducing "An Expert" as opposed to saying, "Please welcome Someone who simply wants to talk for 45 minutes," my gut still tightens anytime the term is used in reference to me.

It just seems to go against everything I believe as a woman, as a friend, as a wife, as a mother, and as a believer in Christ. After all, I'm the speaker and the writer who loves nothing more than to open her life up for all to see and declare, "I am a mess of magnificent proportions!"

That's the kind of expert I am.

I display special skill at saying the wrong thing at the wrong time. At promising too much and delivering too little—all with the best intentions in mind. *(It's kind of like falling asleep during a sermon or forgetting your notes for a speech.)*

This is why I'm so thankful the trajectory of your life isn't all up to me.

This is why I'm so thankful I don't feel like I have to have all the answers as I write these chatty messages of grace, forgiveness, and hope to you.

This is why I am so thankful it's not about me—and *all* about Scripture.

Do you want to be a woman who trusts God more? Then put down this book and read some expert Scriptures.

"Examine yourselves as to whether you are in the faith. Test yourselves. Do you not know yourselves, that Jesus Christ is in you?" (2 Corinthians 13:5, NKJV)

"Trust God from the bottom of your heart; don't try to figure out everything on your own. Listen for God's voice in everything you do, everywhere you go; he's the one who will keep you on track." (Proverbs 3:5-6)

"God is our refuge and strength, a very present help in trouble." (Psalm 46:1, NKJV)

"Be strong and of good courage; do not be afraid, nor be dismayed, for the Lord your God is with you wherever you go." (Joshua 1:9, NKJV)

Do you want to find out more about hope and heaven? Then read more about it in some expert Scriptures.

"But store up for yourselves treasures in heaven, where neither moth nor rust destroys, and where thieves do not break in or steal." (Matthew 6:20, NASB)

"Not everyone who says to Me, 'Lord, Lord,' will enter the kingdom of heaven, but he who does the will of My Father who is in heaven will enter." (Matthew 7:21, NASB)

"Jesus presented another parable to them, saying, 'The kingdom of heaven may be compared to a man who sowed good seed in his field.'" (Matthew 13:24, NASB)

"And there is salvation in no one else; for there is no other name under heaven that has been given among men by which we must be saved." (Acts 4:12, NASB)

Do you want to answer the questions of "Are we there yet?" as they relate to troubles you face, family you love, and worries you just can't seem to let go? Then read more, lots more, about doing just that in the expert Scriptures.

"Do not worry then, saying, 'What will we eat?' or 'What will we drink?' or 'What will we wear for clothing?'" (Matthew 6:31, NASB)

"If then you cannot do even a very little thing, why do you worry about other matters?" (Luke 12:26, NASB)

"So do not worry about tomorrow; for tomorrow will care for itself. Each day has enough trouble of its own." (Matthew 6:34, NASB)

"If you then, being evil, know how to give good gifts to your children, how much more will your Father who is in heaven give what is good to those who ask Him!" (Matthew 7:11, NASB)

I attempted this a little over three years ago, and I think I'll do it again. It seems only right after confessing my lack of "start your day off with hope" Scripture and my steady diet of bad news and hopelessness via the Internet news channels.

So here it is, girls: I'm going to refrain from turning on the television or slipping downstairs to my Dell until I've first looked to the hope of Scripture. We'll do it together! You read it here first, so feel free to send an e-mail and ask how I'm doing. I'll tell you—honestly—and we can encourage each other.

MILE MARKER #4: 1 THESSALONIANS 4:13

"But we do not want you to be uninformed, brethren, about those who are asleep, so that you will not grieve, as do the rest who have no hope."[7]

My grandmother instilled within me a love for Jesus as well as a love and hope for his appearing. Now a couple of authors have covered this subject rather thoroughly. Perhaps you've heard of their book series, Left Behind? *(Ah, yes, I see that hand.)*

Well, we're going to dive into the subject in the following chapter, but let me just close out this chapter with the importance of marking this truth in your own life. This life isn't all there is. One day we *will* see Jesus. And while I'm no expert, I do know the promises he has made *(as well as the promises he has kept, namely sending Jesus to this earth in the first place)* regarding an out-of-this-world experience with gravity and God.

You better believe I am ready to go. Be it airborne or through those pearly gates, Jesus, take me away! And anytime you please, thank you very much!

The Blessed Hope of one day being caught up with Jesus may sound crazy, far-fetched, and even a bit old-fashioned to some. But those of us who long for his appearing are listening for that telltale sound. We're waiting with great anticipation to see the Someone we love in heaven—the Someone who loves us with an unfathomable amount of love.

This hope, indeed, is life itself.

Nothing less.

Nothing greater.

* 8 *

Going Up!

Sometimes I look at this world around me *(pooh, sometimes I just look at the laundry around me)*, and I find myself getting homesick for another time and another place.

Another time and place where VISA cards, menopause, and *(as far as I know)* droopy body parts do not exist and, better still, don't enter the equation of life eternal.

Another time and place where all the loose ends of life will truly be tied up.

Another time and place where our faith and hope will be made sight, and with that sight we will see God.[1]

I want to experience in my lifetime that marvelous occurrence always referred to as "The Rapture" as I was growing up. Our friend the apostle Paul *(for he is indeed our friend—this man who has taught us so much about divine grace and forgiveness. Perhaps because he experienced it so deeply himself?)*—also points us toward The One who embodies all hope for now and eternity. Over 2,000 years ago, Paul boldly proclaimed to believers and friends living in Greece the same message he wants us to hear today:

"And then this: We can tell you with complete confidence—we have the Master's word on it—that when the Master comes again to get us, those of us who are still alive will not get a jump on the dead and leave them behind. In actual fact, they'll be ahead of us. The Master himself will give the command. Archangel thunder! God's trumpet blast! He'll come down from heaven and the dead in Christ will rise—they'll go first. Then the rest of us who are still alive at the time will be caught up with them into the clouds to meet the Master. Oh, we'll be walking on air! And then there will be one huge family reunion with the Master. So reassure one another with these words."[2]

My grandma often referred to the Rapture as "the blessed hope."[3] She would talk about it often and with great enthusiasm. Not a wacky, "Grandma, you're scaring me" type of enthusiasm but an unshakable and enviable trust and confidence in something that was sure to come. I can't read the preceding paragraph without thinking of her and a Southern Gospel music group that went by the name of The John Matthews Family.

When I was about nine years old, Grandma took me to a concert to hear that group sing and also purchased a 76 RPM record of their music for me to take home. This is how I memorized the preceding Bible verses—through the melody of a song. I can close my eyes and "hear" the lead singer's voice declaring, "And we, who are alive, shall be caught up in the air, and so shall we EVER be with the Lord!"

Those are some shouting words of hope, girls!

Throughout my childhood, the eternal hope of seeing Jesus was being massaged and nurtured through Bible teaching and great music. I would attend church and listen and sing great song standards such as "When the Roll Is Called Up Yonder," "When We All Get to Heaven," as well as the first, second, and last verse of "Oh, Victory in Jesus." *(I'm not sure why it is, but for some reason all the churches I went to as a child left out the third verse of every church hymn. I always felt sorry for that dismissed stanza.)*

And my grandma wasn't the only one who knew a thing or two about this thing called the blessed hope.

Around the age of 14 I got my hands on a beat-up paperback copy of *The Late Great Planet Earth.* Oh, my goodness! Do you remember that book, girls? Its author attempted to explain prophecies about the end of the world and to predict, more or less, when that end would occur.

It was a humdinger of a read, especially for a teenage girl, and it put my Nancy Drew mystery books to shame—as well as any James Patterson types I had hidden from my mother. *Late Great Planet* was filled with all manner of foreboding warnings of impending judgment against planet Earth. After reading about nations fighting with nations, bad guys doing bad things, and flat-out evil becoming more and more the norm, well, I was standing on tiptoe just begging for heaven, Jesus, and the Rapture.

It also convinced me that my freshman basketball coach was indeed the Antichrist.

Really.

He met all the requirements. . . .

✳ He was mean. *(He never called me by my first or last name. He simply pointed at me and said, "You, stand there.")*

✳ He was evil. *(What else could a man be who demanded we run 12 wind sprints in one practice? Evil, pure evil, I tell you.)*

✳ And there was that highly suspicious mark on his head. *(No one was quite sure where it came from, but we all had our theories.)*

Then again, come to think of it, I may be getting him confused with Damien from the 1970s movie thriller, *The Omen. (For the real deal regarding such matters, just read Revelation 13.)*

Never mind.

Late Great was the first of many books to pique my interest in the blessed hope. There was also *Raptured! Raptured! Raptured!*—a book I found under an avalanche of cut-out magazine recipes in the round lampstand at Grandma's house. That book was a bit over the top, in my opinion. I could have used some good counseling after finishing it, what with all the persecution and mayhem that awaited those who had not made it in the first go-around *(a.k.a., "The Rapture").*

I have a close friend who was raised in a denomination quite different from the one I grew up in. While she was taught about Jesus and heard Bible stories about who he was and why he came to earth, she had never been exposed to the concept of the Rapture.

"It sounds, well, a bit crazy if you ask me," she told me several years ago.

And I agreed.

When you break it down and think about it in limited, finite terms, it does indeed sound like some script written for the once-popular television series *The X-Files.* It isn't hard to imagine the show's chief characters, Fox Mulder and Dana Scully, investigating claims of dead people being raised from graves[4] and the mass disappearance of men, women, and children who all held to a belief in Jesus Christ. It isn't hard to imagine Fox Mulder *(played by actor David Duchovny)* repeating over and over again, "The truth is out there."

I think that's why I always liked that show so much. It intrigued me because I, too, believe that "the truth is out there." And it's out there for those who believe in Jesus already, as well as for those who are curious and investigating who Jesus claims to be. And Jesus, too, is watching what our response will be.

Fox, like so many of us, wanted to believe in something and Someone apart from what he could see visibly and touch tangibly.

Like so many of us, Fox was holding on to hope.

Let me encourage you to let yourself do just that while reading this chapter.

Let yourself believe in what you cannot see.

Let yourself hope in something beyond the confines of human imagination.

Let your mind wrap its way around perhaps an entirely new prospect of grace, redemption, and hope—that of being carried away to heaven and Jesus without ever having to experience death.

(I'm all over that option.)

In fact, I believe right now would be an excellent time for him to call us up in the clouds. *(Funny how this thought always comes around book deadline time.)*

I think I've alluded to my admittedly sometimes less-than-noble motivations regarding such matters in previous books. You may recall in *Radical Forgiveness* my prayers of, "Dear Jesus, you know I love you and want to see you but . . .

> . . . could you wait until I get to date?"
> . . . could you wait until I have sex?"
> . . . could you wait until I have children?"

Well, now that I'm a good 25 years down the road since then, my prayers regarding the Rapture have changed slightly. They go a bit more like this. . . .

"Dear Lord Jesus, please come *now* . . .

> . . . before I have three children in college."
> . . . before I go through menopause."
> . . . before my chest droops any farther."
> . . . before my VISA card bill arrives."

So there you go.

I know my motives may not always be the purest. But when all is said and done, ladies, it really does come down to me looking forward with hope to one day seeing Jesus face-to-face.

So, yes, I agree with my friend who says the idea of the Rapture sounds crazy. But this is where that virtuous trio of faith, love, and hope comes into play. It is by *faith* that we believe in what cannot be seen. It is *love*—divine love—that compels us to Jesus. And it is *hope* that keeps our ears trained for the sound of a trumpet!

Believing the Rapture could happen seems no crazier a

thought than believing God sent Jesus to planet Earth in the first place. It seems no crazier than believing God delights in having a relationship with us as a result of what Jesus did.

No crazier than *not* to believe. And really, what do you have to lose? Why would you not choose to go through life with hope rather than cynicism?

However, in order for you to believe, even in the midst of difficult circumstances, you'll need some sturdy, enduring truths to buoy up your faith. It isn't enough for you to read about my personal accounts or take the word of other authors or speakers.

No, just like grace and forgiveness, hope must become yours. It must be rooted in truth. And, ladies, the only truth I am willing to bet my life upon is the truth that has been revealed to us through the message of the Bible, the enduring Word of God. And it is that truth of Scripture that provides buoys of hope as we look forward to what is to come.

BUOY OF TRUTH #1: JESUS PROMISED HE WOULD RETURN FOR US.

"Don't let this throw you. You trust God, don't you? Trust me. There is plenty of room for you in my Father's home. If that weren't so, would I have told you that I'm on my way to get a room ready for you? And if I'm on my way to get your room ready, I'll come back and get you so you can live where I live."[5]

"I'm telling you these things while I'm still living with you. The Friend, the Holy Spirit whom the Father will send at my request, will make everything plain to you. He will remind you of all the things I have told you. I'm leaving you well and whole. That's my parting gift

to you. Peace. I don't leave you the way you're used to being left—
feeling abandoned, bereft. So don't be upset. Don't be distraught.

"You've heard me tell you, 'I'm going away and I'm coming back.' If
you loved me, you would be glad that I'm on my way to the Father
because the Father is the goal and purpose of my life.

"I've told you this ahead of time, before it happens, so that when it
does happen, the confirmation will deepen your belief in me. I'll not
be talking with you much more like this because the chief of this god-
less world is about to attack. But don't worry—he has nothing on me,
no claim on me. But so the world might know how thoroughly I love
the Father, I am carrying out my Father's instructions right down to
the last detail."[6]

The Rapture will be the fulfillment of the promise Jesus made to
his disciples during his last meal with them. His promise to return
for them (as well as all believers who have trusted him as Savior)
was a kiss of peace upon their troubled and perplexed brows.

Just try to picture it.

Jesus is speaking to 11 of his most trusted and loved friends
*(Judas had already left the building to seal his deal with those who
sought to capture and kill Jesus)* and trying to get them to understand the magnitude of what lies ahead for all of them.

Betrayal.

Fear.

Accusation.

Murder.

And seeming hopelessness.

Within hours, Judas would place a traitorous kiss against the
face of God.

Within hours, Peter—loud, passionate, and confident Peter—
would deny he even knew Jesus. Not one, not two, but three
curse-filled times.

Within hours, Jesus would be disfigured by the fists and
whips of man.

Within hours, those 11 men who loved Jesus and believed
him to be the Promised One of Israel would scatter and flee.

Within hours all hope, it would seem, would be lost.

Try and picture it. . . .

Yet, in the midst of knowing the horror and pain that awaited
him, Jesus took the time—and oh, what a grace-filled time it
was!—to speak words of hope to these men whom he loved.
To place a grace-filled kiss of "going up!" hope on the brows
of each of us, the women for whom he suffered and died.

Do you see how hope intertwines and weaves in and out of
itself? We have this hope—this blessed hope of Christ's return-
based upon a promise made thousands of years ago. We can
hold to the buoy of this hope, for it is woven into the uncompro-
mising truth that tells us (see p. 27) God cannot lie.

Jesus is the Author of this truth.

Not Tim LaHaye or Jerry Jenkins.

Not slightly scary Hal Lindsey.

Not the *really* scary author of that book I read long, long ago.

Jesus said it.

Boldly. Plainly. Confidently.

And in the hour before the most painful time in his existence.

He can't lie.

He will return.

So get ready!

BUOY OF TRUTH #2: THE RAPTURE IS ANOTHER
MYSTERY REVEALED.

In Chapter 2 I told you the apostle Paul had revealed another mystery apart from "Christ in you, the hope of glory." But I wouldn't tell you what it was. Well, this is it, ladies! *(Note: Don't fasten your seat belts, however. I want you to be completely loose and ready if that trumpet sounds while reading this paragraph!)*

"ʙut let me tell you something wonderful, a mystery I'll probably never fully understand. We're not all going to die—*but* we are all going to be changed. You hear a blast to end all blasts from a trumpet, and in the time that you look up and blink your eyes—it's over. On signal from that trumpet from heaven, the dead will be up and out of their graves, beyond the reach of death, never to die again. At the same moment and in the same way, we'll all be changed. In the resurrection scheme of things, this has to happen: everything perishable taken off the shelves and replaced by the imperishable, this mortal replaced by the immortal. Then the saying will come true:

Death swallowed by triumphant Life!

Who got the last word, oh, Death?

Oh, Death, who's afraid of you now?

It was sin that made death so frightening and law-code guilt that gave sin its leverage, its destructive power. But now in a single victorious stroke of Life, all three—sin, guilt, death—are gone, the gift of our Master, Jesus Christ. Thank God!"[7]

Oh! Don't you see how this promise, this mystery, can only be tied up in Jesus?! Dear friend, how I want you to desire and long for the sound of that trumpet just as I do!

It may sound cheesy, but my heart truly does "leap" within me when I read these Bible verses. I close my eyes and just imagine *(again, because Jesus said it would happen and he can't lie)* the day when I'm going about my own business, maybe writing another book or putting away mismatched socks *(I quit trying to match them up about four years ago)* in my children's dresser drawers, when it happens. . . .

A trumpet blasts!

My head instinctively lifts to the sound, and before I can even lift my eyes up, I've left those socks behind! *(I wonder if Mr. Jenkins thought of the glory that would bring to women all across the universe?)*

And in that same moment (*"from quantum physics consider-ations, it is suspected that this transformation, 'in the twinkling of an eye,' will occur digitally in 10/43 of a second"*[8]) we will be with Jesus.

"Inconceivable!" as the character Vizzini would sputter from *The Princess Bride.*

Inconceivable, but true.

This hope we have as an anchor, ladies. This hope we have as a buoy against the waves of frustration and routine. This hope we have as a constant reminder of what will be.

I tell you what—once this mystery takes hold of your heart and you grab this buoy of truth, you'll never hear train whistles or siren blasts the same again.

It wasn't long after Rick and I had moved into our house in Illinois that it happened. I was dead asleep—as close as you can get to being alive but totally out of it—but I "heard" a trumpet blast.

My spirit "heard" a trumpet blast.

My hope "heard" a trumpet blast.

And before you could say, *"deinde nos qui vivimus qui relinquimur simul rapiemur cum illis in nubibus obviam Domino in aera et sic semper cum Domino erimus" (that's the Latin translation of 1 Thessalonians 4:17),* I sat up, wide awake, and anxiously waited for my transfer out of Prairie City.

Alas, it was but the whistle blast of a passing Amtrak passenger train.

But boy, did it feel good to hope this was it!

BUOY OF TRUTH #3: IT COULD HAPPEN IN OUR LIFETIME.
Just like us, the disciples were curious as to when Jesus would return. They asked him what they could look for and how they could know when it was near. Here's what Jesus said:

"Take a lesson from the fig tree. From the moment you notice its buds form, the merest hint of green, you know summer's just around the corner. So it is with you: When you see all these things, you'll know he's at the door. Don't take this lightly. I'm not just saying this for some future generation, but for all of you. This age continues until all these things take place. Sky and earth will wear out; my words won't wear out.

"But the exact day and hour? No one knows that, not even heaven's angels, not even the Son. Only the Father knows.

"The Arrival of the Son of Man will take place in times like Noah's. Before the great flood everyone was carrying on as usual, having a good time right up to the day Noah boarded the ark. They knew nothing—until the flood hit and swept everything away.

"The Son of Man's Arrival will be like that: Two men will be working in the field—one will be taken, one left behind; two women will be grinding at the mill—one will be taken, one left behind. So stay awake, alert. You have no idea what day your Master will show up. But you do know this: You know that if the homeowner had known what time of night the burglar would arrive, he would have been there with his dogs to prevent the break-in. Be vigilant just like that. You have no idea when the Son of Man is going to show up."⁹

"Jesus is coming soon, morning or night or noon"—that's the hymn I remember singing as a young girl, and it's the cry of my heart as I look at the world around me. Jesus also told the disciples to watch for religious leaders eager to say, "I am the Christ." He warned us of such leaders' deceptive power and encouraged them to keep their wits about them as they heard reports of wars and rumors of wars.

"When reports come in of wars and rumored wars, keep your head and don't panic. . . . Nation will fight nation and ruler fight ruler, over and over. Famines and earthquakes will occur in various places. This is nothing compared to what is coming."¹⁰

Jesus likened all the warning signs pointing to the catching away of believers to those of labor pains. As a woman draws closer and closer to delivery, her contractions increase. With each contraction there comes more intense pain, but also the glorious promise of new life.

This is how I must look at the warning signs.

Remember, I'm the information guru of Illinois, and the more I know, the more anxious I get at times. But that's not the way

Jesus wants us to think of the future. As I read and see evidence of the earth's birthing pangs—its desire to give birth to the mystery of his coming to Earth again—I should be lifting my head with hope rather than looking for a cave to hide in!

Every contraction draws Christ all the more near.

So when I read of a self-appointed group in Jerusalem, calling themselves "the Sanhedrin" (leaders of the Jewish court system) and desiring to appoint a King of Israel, I lift my head up and hope for the true King to come.

When I watch The Weather Channel and hear announcers stymied by ever-changing weather patterns and floods, droughts, hurricanes, and other natural disasters, I lift my head up and hope for The One who is to come.

I don't pack up all my family's belongings and go flee in the mountains of Montana.

I rest.

Yes, rest.

I rest on the shores of exquisite hope, knowing that this *right here, right now* is not all there is.

I rest on the knowledge that God is in control of all events and situations, and I rest in the fact that Jesus will make good on his promise.

He cannot lie.

He said he would return for us.

And he will.

Jesus never breaks his promises. Not once.

When all is shaky around us, Jesus remains firm.

All that remains for you is to decide if you will believe in him.

So, what do you think?

And what do you have to lose?

In Christ we find hope for eternal life and peace for the life we live on Earth. In Christ are hidden exquisite secrets and mysteries—all revealed to us through the truth of his message, the Bible.

Wouldn't you like to escape the frazzle of this life and be swept away to another time and another place?

Wouldn't you like to take a pass on walking through the valley of the shadow of death[11] and simply proceed to another time and another place?

Wouldn't you love to join Jesus in that time and place?

All that remains is your asking him to take his rightful place in your life. And when you do, I'd love nothing more than to receive a postcard or e-mail from you *(you'll find my contact information on page 158),* telling me you've planted your chaise lounger on the shores of eternal hope.

Won't you join me there?

I'll Take You There

When's the last time you saw a pink flamingo snow skiing?

Now that I think about it, have you *ever* spied a pink flamingo snow skiing?

Well, if you visit the slopes of a certain mountain in Montana toward the end of every January, you'll see just that. Each year, bobbing and weaving, careening and preening on snow-covered peaks, are approximately 45 women from all walks of life. And they're all adorned in dazzling pink fleece hats that proudly identify them as a gregarious member of The Flamingo Girls.

The Flamingo Girls are a rowdy, righteous, and raucous group of females who've managed to meet two times a year for over 15 years. They are women who know a thing or two about hospitality, falling off toilet seats, and holding on to what truly matters—one another.

On occasion, they allow other gregarious birds into their midst.

Such was the place I found myself in January of 2005.

Now the irony wasn't lost on me that I was about to join 45 complete strangers in the state of Montana, on a ski resort, during the middle of winter. You know my issues with cold and snow—what was I thinking?

Well, if nothing else, I could sit around a fireplace and spout deep and profound thoughts, right?

Er, wrong.

It seems everyone goes to this certain resort during this certain time of year to ski—cross country or downhill.

Huh. I was in a tight spot indeed.

For I immediately had flashbacks to my working out on my NordicTrack cross-country ski machine in 1994. I'll admit it got me in the best shape of my life. I worked off three inches from my waistline, and my thighs took a breather from their otherwise close relationship.

But I could barely track and think at the same time. And as far as speaking? Well, it was entirely out of the question except for periodic outbursts of shouting at my then four-year-old son, Ricky, "Quit riding your tricycle so close to me! I'm going to poke your eyes out!" *(Or something like that.)*

So as I rode from the airport in Montana to where we were lodging, all I could think about was gasping for breath, thighs quivering from lack of use, and me screaming at the stranger next to me, "Quit getting so close to me! I'm going to poke your eyes out!" *(Or something like that.)*

Such a thought then left me with the other option—the outdoor activity of downhill skiing.

Ah, yes, what an excellent idea.

Me, Julie Ann Barnhill, whose only connection with downhill skiing involved the *ABC's Wide World of Sports* camera shot of a man tumbling *(surely)* to his death down a mountainside.

Me, Julie Ann Barnhill, standing on thin waxed strips of a hard material, on a mountain incline, pointing downhill.

Me, Julie Ann Barnhill, who can barely sing and clap to the rhythm of a beat.

So that's what I chose to do. *(Freestyle jacuzzi sitting did not qualify under Flamingo guidelines. Rats!)*

I gave our activities director, Cindy, my shoe and pant size *(as well as weight*)* because I am an all or-nothing chick who, when push comes to shove, refuses to admit she can't do something.

A few hours later I had on a pair of snow boots, two skewers on which to impale myself, and those turkey-sized mittens I mentioned in Chapter 6. I was also meeting the poor guy who drew the short straw and got stuck with a clueless snow newbie like me.

Several minutes before Cindy introduced the instructors for our individual groups, I had begged her to appoint us *(there were two other novice Flamingos with me)* the nicest, most patient, most "willing to go inside the lodge and talk over hot chocolate" instructor there was.

We got Link. And he *was* nice and patient . . . but only willing to share a cup of cocoa *after* we had mastered standing up and actually moving on our skis. Hmm, it looked like the next 14 hours were going to be beverage-free as soon as we made it to the coaching area.

While seasoned Flamingos took off for summits and runs, and my cohorts, Gretchen and Martha, snapped their boots into

---

* I gave her the exact amount too! I figured there was no room for error if it involved me and a ski-lift seat 4,000 feet above the ground.

their skis, I was still trying to get my gloves on. It was going to be a very long day.

Or so I thought.

But within an hour or so, Gretchen had moved on to the skill level above *(basically, Flamingos who aren't facedown in the snow 99.5 percent of the time),* and my buddy Martha had decided to call it a day. *(Who was the smart one, huh?)* So, lo and behold, I found myself to be the recipient of a private ski instructor.

Now that's not going to happen many times in my lifetime, is it?

So my all-or-nothingness kicked in *(especially after swallowing three Aleves for the pain that was sure to come)* and I declared to The Flamingo Girls, Link, and anyone else who would listen, "I'm going to release my inner warrior athletic Flamingo Princess and take that mountain!"

(Someone really should put me out of my drama misery!)

After a few false starts, I found myself on the ski lift heading to the top of the bunny slope—my faithful instructor by my side. But all the while I was thinking, *What on earth are you doing?!*

I managed to get off the lift, despite my forgetting the minor detail of standing up. *(No big deal—I just rolled and writhed my way out of danger as Link tried not to stare with dismay.)* And I slowly made my way to the center of the ski run.

When the "run" was much wider than I thought it would be, I felt much better. It had looked sorta skinny from the bottom of the slope.

I wasn't too worried at all about going down until I skied approximately 18 inches . . . and toppled over. Link said I abused my ski poles *(translation: I attempted to stab the ground and stop my body from plummeting down the bunny slope)* and promptly took them away from me.

I was flummoxed.

Dumbfounded and scared.

Wondering what Rick would think when I phoned him from a hospital in Montana and asked him to come get me.

So I looked at Link and asked, "How *exactly* am I supposed to get down the mountain if I don't have any poles to guide myself with?"

He raised an eyebrow. "Julie, you don't need these ski poles to guide you. All you need to do is trust the things I have taught you, lean into your boots, and simply keep your eyes on where you want to go. Then your body and your skis will follow."

I didn't believe a word he said. It was too much like "Zen thinking" for me. I needed tangible items I could see and touch *(my ski poles, his body skiing backwards in front of me)* to convince me otherwise. But Link wasn't handing over the poles, and we'd already done the backwards ski thing once.

Link truly believed I could ski down by myself.

Sigh.

It was one of those times where you just have to decide to suck it up and do what needs to be done. It was one of those character-building moments—as well as hope-building moments—because I was just hoping I didn't kill myself or someone else on the sure-to-be disastrous trip down.

So I started off *my* way.

I leaned into the skis and tried to force them to go where I wanted . . . and landed on my backside immediately. I only did this once. I'm not stupid, and I'm not unwilling to admit when I am wrong. Just a little headstrong sometimes . . . er, all the time.

So I again asked Link to tell me what to do.

With a patient, "I've been teaching people to ski for over 25 years" smile, Link sagely advised, "Trust what you know, lean into the boots, and look where you want to be—your body and skis will follow. Here, watch me." He moved gracefully across the snow to the left and then the right, turning his gaze only when he desired to change his course. "Now, you do it," he challenged.

And so I did.

I laid aside the false security of ski poles.

I put aside my doubt and Zen advice cynicism.

And instead I trusted what Link had taught me: legs hip-distance apart; skis in a wedge shape and moving as if I were spreading peanut butter with them; leaning into the front of my boots; and fixing my gaze on where I wanted to go.

First locking my eyes on a certain tree *(a tree far removed from the actual path I was making! Again, I remind you . . . I'm not stupid!)*, I found my body skiing toward the left.

Then, moving my head slightly and fixing my gaze on a ski-lift pole far *far* to the right. And what do you know?! My body and skis began to follow.

Side by side.

Left, then right.

Until I found myself at the base of the Easy Rider run, feeling like I'd conquered Mount Everest.

Beaming from ear to ear, Link then swooshed up next to me *(he's got that cool ski thing down solid)*. "You definitely released your inner warrior princess! And never forget, just keep your eyes on where you want to go, and your body and mind will follow."

Who knew ski instructors could be so wise?

(Later we ended up finally having that drink of hot chocolate, and I found out that Link had been everything from a marine biologist in Alaska to a bug specialist in India.)

And who knew my personal ski instructor would give me just the words I needed to finish up one long, overdue chapter to this book!?

I just love it when God does things like that!

I had taken my laptop to Montana in hopes of completing this one chapter. My husband had questioned why I bothered to do so because I never seem to write anything when I actually set out to write something. *(Remember this fact the next time you think of me. Remember and pray! And realize that if I can write, you can do the impossible too!)* But I really didn't have any other choice.

I had wrestled and fought with this chapter for six months and still didn't feel like I had the right words down. I had read scads and scads of Bible verses, prayed a lot, whined more, and kept sending e-mails to my editor, apologizing for not getting it together.

Meanwhile, God was at work.

Meanwhile, exquisite hope was on its way.

You see, Link and I couldn't help but engage in all manner of deep conversations while riding together on the lift *(remember me confessing to diving in when it comes to getting to know someone?)*. After all, this was a guy whom I'd been told had been trained to catch up with an out-of-control skier *(i.e., me)* and throw himself in front of that person to stop him or her safely. That intrigued me. I wanted to know more about a guy who was willing to go to such lengths for me—a virtual stranger.

Anyway, we talked shop and eventually made our way to matters of faith. I listened to his story; he was gracious enough to listen to some of mine. In the midst of it all, I thought how closely Link's advice to me on top of the mountain matched the biblical hope I had somehow missed in writing this chapter on hope.

Read and tell me if you don't see it also:

"**D**o you see what this means—all these pioneers who blazed the way, all these veterans cheering us on? It means we'd better get on with it. Strip down, start running—and never quit! No extra spiritual fat, no parasitic sins. Keep your eyes on *Jesus*, who both began and finished this race we're in. Study how he did it. Because he never lost sight of where he was headed—that exhilarating finish in and with God—he could put up with anything along the way: cross, shame, whatever. And now he's *there*, in the place of honor, right alongside God. When you find yourself flagging in your faith, go over that story again, item by item, that long litany of hostility he plowed through. *That* will shoot adrenaline into your souls! . . . So don't sit around on your hands! No more dragging your feet! Clear the path for long-distance runners so no one will trip and fall, so no one will step in a hole and sprain an ankle. Help each other out. And run for it!"[1]

Somehow over the course of months, I had forgotten The One on whom my eyes are to be fixed. I had managed to set aside the beacon of my hope and failed to remember that God is The One who will make my paths straight in life and in the eternal.

In fact, that's exactly what Hebrews 12:12-13 tells us: "Therefore, strengthen the hands that are weak and the knees that are feeble, and make straight paths for your feet"[2]

When I realign my vision and set my gaze on Jesus—my mind and body will follow.

When I set my eyes on the eternal and The One who is eternal—my desires and motives will follow.

When I purposely choose Jesus to be the Navigational Instructor for my soul—a longing for things eternal will follow.

And nothing is more eternal than the hope of heaven—here, watch me, and let me take you there.

✳ ✳ ✳

"I saw Heaven and earth new-created. Gone the first Heaven, gone the first earth, gone the sea. I saw Holy Jerusalem, new-created, descending resplendent out of Heaven, as ready for God as a bride for her husband. I heard a voice thunder from the Throne: 'Look! Look! God has moved into the neighborhood, making his home with men and women! They're his people, he's their God. He'll wipe every tear from their eyes. Death is gone for good—tears gone, crying gone, pain gone—all the first order of things gone.' The Enthroned continued, 'Look! I'm making everything new. Write it all down—each word dependable and accurate.' Then he said, 'It's happened. I'm A to Z. I'm the Beginning, I'm the Conclusion. From Water-of-Life Well I give freely to the thirsty. Conquerors inherit all this. I'll be God to them, they'll be sons and daughters to me.'"[3]

This is faith and hope made sight, ladies!

This is life as it was purposed to be lived at the dawn of Creation. We were created for friendship with God. The book of
Genesis boldly alludes to the fact that God himself once walked
with man and woman in the Garden of Eden.[4]

Can you even begin to imagine what that must have been like?

To be able to stand beside the Creator of All and enjoy his
company and favor?

To live in such a place as to know no shame, no guilt, no sin,
or regret?

This is where my heart and soul and body longs to be—with
God, wherever he may be.

Remember how we spoke of scorched places in *Scandalous
Grace*? Perhaps, even now, you thirst for refreshment and satis-
faction in those dry, scorched places of the past. Listen to me
and hear my words. Trust what you have been taught *(God is
faithful, loving, and cannot lie)*, fix your gaze on your goal *(Jesus
and heaven)*, and lean into him and trust.

Side by side.

Left to right.

Until you make your way over the course of life and arrive at
your ultimate destination of Hope.

✳ ✳ ✳

You've probably heard the expression, "She couldn't see the
forest for the trees." Well, I want us to direct our gaze to a
Tree—a Tree that embodies and sums up every exquisite ele-
ment of divine hope I have so desired you to embrace.

"Then the Angel showed me Water-of-Life River, crystal bright. It flowed from the Throne of God and the Lamb, right down the middle of the street. The Tree of Life was planted on each side of the River, producing twelve kinds of fruit, a ripe fruit each month. The leaves of the Tree are for healing the nations. Never again will anything be cursed. The Throne of God and of the Lamb is at the center. His servants will offer God service—worshiping, they'll look on his face, their foreheads mirroring God. Never again will there be any night. No one will need lamplight or sunlight. The shining of God, the Master, is all the light anyone needs. And they will rule with him age after age after age."[5]

I know a place where there will be no more wars.

I know a place where there will never be another broken heart.

I know a place where concrete walls and barbed-wire fences will no longer separate the nations.

I know a place where all our longings, all our desires, all our all will be fulfilled and found in The One.

How interesting that the leaves of the tree of life offer healing for God's creation. For in the beginning, in another garden, it was forbidden fruit, eaten from another tree that brought about the need for Jesus. *(How I wish that Adam and Eve had not sampled that fruit, don't you? But we cannot change history . . .)*

If you asked me why I believe in God, in Jesus, and in the hope of a place called Heaven, it would be for this reason alone: God always wraps up what he started. From Adam and Eve to that final tear wiped from its beloved owner's face, God wraps up what he started.

This is why I believe in a place called Hope.

This is why I have confident expectation in The One.

This is why I find myself smiling and humming what will surely be my song throughout the ages:

> *Holy, Holy, Holy!*
> *Lord God Almighty!*
> *Early in the morning our songs shall rise to Thee.*
> *Holy, holy, holy!*
> *merciful and mighty,*
> *God in three persons, blessed Trinity.*

> *Holy, holy, holy!*
> *all the saints adore Thee*
> *Casting down their golden crowns*
> *around the glassy sea;*
> *Cherubim and seraphim*
> *falling down before Thee*
> *Which wert and art and evermore shalt be.*[6]

Can you see yourself standing by the shores of that river, girls?

Can you imagine what it will be like to see the face of The One who has lavished us with his grace, rescued us with his Cross, and purposed us to live forever and forever *(totally beyond my ability to comprehend)* with him?

One of my favorite quotes regarding this journey of faith we're all engaged in is found in *The Westminster Confessions* and reads as such: "The end purpose of man [woman] is to love God, worship him and enjoy him forever."[7]

You can rest on the shores of this hope, my friend.

Don't worry about grabbing your day planner and filling your minutes with things to do, places to go, and people to see.

Don't beat yourself over the head with a list of shoulds, coulds, woulds, and what-ifs.

Don't don the skis of self-sufficiency and attempt to ski down the mountains of life on your own.

Just stay where you've been the past few hours or days as you've read this book. Relax on the shores of grace and forgiveness and continue to fix your eyes on Jesus alone. *He* is the author of our faith as well as our future, and only he can be trusted to lead us to a place of healing and joy.

Until We Meet Again

Would you look at the tan I got while being here with you?!

We really should do this more often, you know. Say, every 15 months or so. It doesn't seem that long ago that we were first meeting over waving hankies and then, before you know it, I'm wrapping up the final chapter for *Exquisite Hope*.

Ah, Shakespeare was right: Parting *is* such sweet sorrow.

But I've convinced my editor to give me just a few more pages before we need to fold up our towels, throw away the Ho Ho wrappers, and head back to the mainland full of responsibilities, traffic jams, and a pair of brand-new jeans put in the clothes washer with all the family's white undergarments. *(Yes, all my bras are blue now!)*

This three-book series has been an amazing opportunity for me as a writer and speaker—but more importantly, it has allowed me to get into the heads and hearts of women who, for better or worse, are an awful lot like me.

And you'll never know what a most comforting thought that has been on more days than you can ever imagine. See, I bring all my quirks, insecurities, and expectations for absolute failure to the keyboard each and every time I sit down to write. In fact, they all pull up a chair and make themselves comfortable while I stare blankly at the screen or click my mouse over to Rapture-worthy Web sites like www.templemountfaithful.org.

Sometimes I don't even get that much accomplished.

I rearrange file folders.

Or I pick the makeup out from around the microphone portion of my cell phone.

And sometimes I simply type xxxxxxxx's until they fill a page or two.

I used to e-mail my agent for creative advice *(he usually said, "Um, why don't you quit e-mailing me and just write the book?"),* but then he got a different job *(I'm sure I had nothing to do with his decision to move on)* and my e-mails have been getting bounced back ever since.

Hmm.

When I actually get a book written, well, girls, there is cause for celebration in the Barnhill family home! And that's just what I've been able to do as a result of getting to know you over the course of these three books. Your letters, e-mails, phone calls, and personal comments have acted as a soothing balm of connection and meaning between my fears and God's faithfulness to show up in both our lives.

If you don't mind waiting here with me by the shore for just a few more minutes, I'd like to share a few of those preposterous, sweeping, detailed moments of the Divine, for they are the stories of our lives.

✳ I just finished the chapter "The Other Woman." That is SOOOO me! You have given me permission to accept myself—but without making excuses for attitudes and behaviors that are destructive.

Not too long ago, I was speaking at a women's conference when a woman approached me, stopped short, and sized me up from head to toe. Looking me straight in the eye she asked, "Are you Julie Ann Barnhill?"

I wasn't sure I wanted to answer, based on her body language. I confirmed her suspicions as she then inquired, "Have you lost weight?"

Hmm, this was turning into some kind of a conversation.

I confirmed her suspicions yet again. *(After all, it was 2004. Remember my theory of weight loss? Gain weight on odd years, lose weight on even?)*

She scanned me yet again and then said, "Well, that's no fair! Now you're the 'Other Woman' for me! I can't come to any of your workshops today." And she turned and walked away

I'm going to make a point of seeing that woman this year, if she's at that women's conference. After all, it's 2005—and 14 pounds of Exquisite Fudge later.

✳ I thought I was the only one who weighed myself every day, had the stomach in the front—you know, all those things we women beat ourselves up about. Anyway, the reason for the e-mail is, I took the book back to the library without copying the recipe for the angel food cake and the frosting. Can you believe it? I must have this recipe! Would you be so kind as to e-mail it to me?

I gladly e-mailed the recipe, but I thought it might be nice to include it here for any of those who may have missed it the first time.

GRANDMA BONNIE'S TO-DIE-FOR ANGEL FOOD CAKE

1 cup of cake flour (Grandma preferred Swan's Down brand)
1½ cups white sugar
13 egg whites
1½ teaspoons vanilla extract
1½ teaspoons cream of tartar
½ teaspoon salt

Preheat the oven to 375 degrees. Be sure your 10" tube pan is clean and dry. Any amount of oil or residue could deflate the egg whites. Sift together the flour and ¾ cup of the sugar; set aside.

In a large bowl, whip the egg whites along with the vanilla, cream of tartar, and salt, until they form medium-stiff peaks. Gradually add the remaining sugar (2 tablespoons at a time) while continuing to whip to stiff peaks. When the egg mixture has reached its maximum volume, fold in the sifted ingredients gradually, one third at a time. Do not overmix. Pour the batter into ungreased tube pan. Gently cut through batter with metal spatula to ensure uniformity of batter.

Bake for 40–45 minutes in the preheated oven until the cake springs back when touched. Balance the tube pan upside down on its legs to prevent decompression while cooling. If your pan does not have these "legs," simply balance it over a couple of cans. When cool, run a knife around the edge of the pan and invert onto a plate or platter.

ICING

2 8-ounce packages cream cheese, softened
(do not substitute with low-fat cheese)
½ cup butter, softened (do not substitute with margarine)

¼ cup half-and-half
2 teaspoons vanilla
5½ cups powdered sugar
1 tablespoon lemon juice (optional)

Beat cream cheese and butter until light and fluffy. Beat in vanilla. Gradually add powdered sugar. Add half-and-half to desired texture and add lemon juice if desired. Lavish cake when it is completely cooled. Enjoy!

And while we're at it, ladies, just in case after the Exquisite Fudge, you have another chocolate urge, and you've loaned *Radical Forgiveness* to a friend, you might need that recipe too. So here goes. . . .

DIVINE DOUBLE CHOCOLATE-CHIP COOKIES

Beat with electric mixer until creamy:
1 cup butter
⅔ cup white sugar
⅔ cup brown sugar
1 teaspoon vanilla
2 eggs

Then add:

2 cups flour
¾ cup baking cocoa
1 teaspoon baking soda
½ teaspoon salt

Beat until creamy again. Stir in 2 cups chocolate chips. Drop by spoonfuls (or use cookie scoop) onto ungreased cookie sheets.

Bake at 350 degrees for 9–11 minutes until firm. Let stand for 2 minutes. Remove to wire racks to cool completely.

✳ I snorted and laughed my way through *Scandalous Grace* in record time. My life has been hectic lately so I REALLY needed to relax. I got your book as a good way to kick-start my summer. I had no idea how much I NEEDED to hear what this book had to say.

Scandalous Grace gave us an excellent foundation to build this friendship upon. I put my heart out on paper, and you accepted and identified with the good and the bad. I can't imagine anything better happening.

I just want you to know how much I appreciate each and every bit of correspondence and feedback. For this is more—so much more—than simply buying a book or my thinking of one more thing to ramble on about.

No, *Scandalous* is about you knowing—beyond a shadow of a doubt—that you are not alone in your foibles and fun, or your scorched places and grief. Like this woman who shared her heart:

Sometime last year I sent you a doozy of a letter. You responded personally, encouraging me to call you. But I couldn't. Too much pride, I guess. That feeling of dumping on another individual is hard for me. I also had visions of someone feeling sorry for me and having compassion for me, which I don't feel I deserve.

Anyway, I went out and bought a copy of Ragamuffin Gospel, as you recommended, and mostly bathed in the love and grace of God. This past weekend in Nashville, I was able to hear you again, this time on the scandalous grace of

God. All throughout the weekend I just kept seeing/hearing the theme that it is just ALL ABOUT HIM, and it is not about me. Sometimes it's hard for me to grasp how that plays out in real life . . . but the fact remains. I need to stay connected to the Lord, to be reminded of his grace toward me (no matter my continual failings), to be faithful to be in the Word, to be real, to be obedient to him, because in the end (and the beginning and middle too) it is all about HIM and for his glory.

I know all these things, but I continue to struggle. Some days are better than others. I still struggle with depression, mood swings, anger, and a host of other problems . . . sometimes to the point of exhaustion. But then I look to the Lord, scrape myself off the floor, and remind myself of what I know to be true of God, his character, his love, his promises, his forgiveness, his grace. And truth is better than fiction (or feelings).

Can you find yourself swimming somewhere in the words of this sweet woman? Have you ever hesitated to reach out for help because of pride or fear of sounding and looking too needy?

Me too.

That's why I wanted to wrap up our time together with your stories. For we are all far more alike than we are different—be it as authors, readers, stay-at-home moms, single women, or 80-year-old girlfriends hanging out in front of airport vanity mirrors.

The palate of the Divine colors every area of our life with the strokes of grace, forgiveness, and hope. And I am so thankful you have allowed me to be a small part of his lavish working in your life.

It's beginning to get a bit chilly, so I guess it's time I pulled up my lounger and let you go back home. Why don't we agree to meet here again sometime? In fact, let's do just that and bring another friend or two along with us! What do you say?

I'll bring the important things, like chocolate and the greatest hits of Huey Lewis and the News, and you—well, you can just promise to show up with that same sense of expectancy as you have before.

Oh, and bring an extra box of Ho Hos, just in case we need 'em.

> *And now to him who can keep you on your feet,*
> *standing tall in his bright presence, fresh and celebrating—*
> *to our one God, our only Savior,*
> *through Jesus Christ, our Master,*
> *be glory, majesty, strength, and rule*
> *before all time, and now, and to the end of all time.*
> *Yes.* [1]

Until we meet again, ladies. . . .

Exquisite Hope Perceived

These quotes have acted as stepping-stones on my own journey toward understanding God's exquisite hope. Perhaps they'll do the same for you.

My aim is to raise hopes by pointing the way to life without end. This is the life God promised long ago—and he doesn't break promises! **TITUS 1:2,** *The Message,* 2174

But blessed is the man who trusts in the Lord, whose confidence is in him. **JEREMIAH 17:7, NIV**

I'm glad from the inside out, ecstatic; I've pitched my tent in the land of hope. **ACTS 2:26,** *The Message,* 1970

If for all practical purposes we believe that this life is our best shot at happiness, if this is as good as it gets, we will live as desperate, demanding, and eventually despairing men and women. We will place on this world a burden it was never intended to bear. . . . All our addictions and depressions, the rage that simmers just beneath the surface of our Christian facade, and the deadness that characterizes so much of our lives has a common root: We think this is as good as it

gets. Take away the hope of arrival and our journey becomes the Battan death march. The best human life is unspeakably sad. Even if we manage to escape some of the bigger tragedies (and few of us do), life rarely matches our expectations. When we do get a taste of what we really long for, it never lasts. Every vacation eventually comes to an end. Friends move away. Our careers don't quite pan out. Sadly, we feel guilty about our disappointment, as though we ought to be more grateful. Of course we're disappointed—we're made for so much more. . . . Our longing for heaven whispers to us in our disappointments and screams through our agony.
BRENT CURTIS AND JOHN ELDREDGE, *The Sacred Romance*

"Hope to the last!" said Newman, clapping him on the back. "Always hope; that's dear boy. Never leave off hoping; it don't answer. Do you mind me, Nick? It don't answer. Don't leave a stone unturned. It's always something, to know you've done the most you could. But, don't leave off hoping, or it's of no use doing anything. Hope, hope, to the last!" **CHARLES DICKENS,** *Nicholas Nickleby*

There is no medicine like hope, no incentive so great, and no tonic so powerful as expectation of something tomorrow. **O. S. MARDEN**

Hope is to our spirits what oxygen is to our lungs. Lose hope and you die. They may not bury you for awhile, but without hope you are dead inside. The only way to face the future is to fly straight into it on the wings of hope. . . . Hope is the energy of the soul. Hope is the power of tomorrow. **LEWIS B. SMEDES**

Now may the God of hope fill you with all joy and peace in believing, so that you will abound in hope by the power of the Holy Spirit.
ROMANS 15:13, NASB

The eternal God is your refuge, and underneath are the everlasting arms. **DEUTERONOMY 33:27, NIV**

And this is what he promised us—even eternal life. **1 JOHN 2:25, NIV**

Hope begins in the dark; the stubborn hope that if you just show up and try to do the right thing, the dawn will come. You wait and watch and work: you don't give up.
ANNE LAMOTT

Go confidently in the directions of your dreams. . . . Live the life you have imagined. **HENRY DAVID THOREAU**

We should all be concerned about the future because we will have to spend the rest of our lives there. **CHARLES FRANKLIN KETTERING**

There have been times when I think we do not desire heaven; but more often I find myself wondering whether, in our heart of hearts, we have ever desired anything else. . . . It is the secret signature of each soul, the incommunicable and unappeasable want, the thing we desired before we met our wives or chose our work, and which we shall still desire on our deathbeds, when the mind no longer knows wife or friend or work. . . . All your life an unattainable ecstasy has hovered just beyond the grasp of your consciousness. The day is coming when you will wake to find, beyond all hope, that you have attained it, or else, that it was within your reach and you have lost it forever.
C. S. LEWIS, The Problem of Pain

Therefore we do not lose heart. Though outwardly we are wasting away, yet inwardly we are being renewed day by day. For our light and momentary troubles are achieving for us an eternal glory that far outweighs them all. **2 CORINTHIANS 4:16-17, NIV**

Then Paul, knowing that some of them were Sadducees and the others Pharisees, called out in the Sanhedrin, "My brothers, I am a Pharisee, the son of a Pharisee. I stand on trial because of my hope in the resurrection of the dead." **ACTS 23:6, NIV**

He who was seated on the throne said, "I am making everything new!" **REVELATION 21:5, NIV**

We fear and hope at the same time. Fear lurks behind hope the way the dark side of the moon lurks behind its shining face. And hope answers fear the way the sun answers the darkness of night. An ordinary visit to the doctor is a little parable of fear and hope. Fear says, "Don't go. You may get bad news." Hope says, "Go, he may find a way to help you." **LEWIS B. SMEDES**

While there's life, there's hope! **Ancient Roman saying**

We can be sure that heaven in the sense of our afterlife is just our future in this universe. There is not another universe besides this one. God created the heavens and earth. That's it. And much of the difficulty in having a believable picture of heaven and hell today comes from the centuries-long tendency to "locate" them in "another reality" outside the created universe. . . . If there is anything we know about the "physical" universe, it surely is that it would be quite adequate to eternal purposes. We may be sure that our life—yes, that familiar one we are each so well acquainted with—will never stop. We should be anticipating what we will be doing three hundred or a thousand or ten thousand years from now in this marvelous universe. **DALLAS WILLARD,** Divine Conspiracy

Hope is the feeling you have that the feeling you have isn't permanent. **JEAN KERR**

For most Christians, heaven is a backup plan. Our primary work is finding a life we can at least get a little pleasure from here. Heaven is an investment like Treasury bonds or a retirement account, which we're hoping will take care of us in the future sometime, but which we do not give much thought to at the present. It's tucked away in a drawer at the back of our minds, while we throw our immediate energies into playing the stock market.
JOHN ELDREDGE, *The Journey of Desire*

But in keeping with his promise we are looking forward to a new heaven and a new earth, the home of righteousness.
2 PETER 3:13, NIV

O Israel, put your hope in the Lord, for with the Lord is unfailing love and with him is full redemption. **PSALM 130:7, NIV**

May your unfailing love rest upon us, O Lord, even as we put our hope in you. **PSALM 33:22, NIV**

Ah! But a man's reach should exceed his grasp! Or what's a heaven for?
ROBERT BROWNING

True hope is swift, and flies with swallow's wings.
WILLIAM SHAKESPEARE, *King Richard III*

Your place in heaven will seem to be made for you and you alone, because you were made for it, made for it stitch by stitch as a glove is made for a hand. **C. S. LEWIS,** *The Problem of Pain*

The very least you can do in your life is to figure out what you hope for. And the most you can do is live inside that hope. Not admire it from a distance but live right in it, under its roof.
BARBARA KINGSOLVER

But when the kindness and love of God our Savior appeared, he saved us, not because of righteous things we had done, but because of his mercy . . . so that, having been justified by his grace, we might become heirs having the hope of eternal life. **TITUS 3:4-5, 7, NIV**

Be strong and take heart, all you who hope in the Lord.
PSALM 31:24, NIV

And we rejoice in the hope of the glory of God. Not only so, but we also rejoice in our sufferings, because we know that suffering produces perseverance; perseverance, character; and character, hope. And hope does not disappoint us, because God has poured out his love into our hearts by the Holy Spirit, whom he has given us. **ROMANS 5:2-5, NIV**

If I find in myself a desire which no experience in this world can satisfy, the most probable explanation is that I was made for another world. If none of my earthly pleasures satisfy it, that does not prove the universe is a fraud. Probably earthly pleasures were never meant to satisfy it, but only arouse it, to suggest the real thing. If that is so, I must take care, on the one hand, never to despise, or be unthankful for, these earthly blessings, and on the other, never to mistake them for the something else of which they are only a kind of copy, or echo, or mirage. I must keep alive in myself the desire for my true country, which I shall not find till after death; I must never let it get snowed under or turned aside; I must make it the main object of life to press on to that other country and to help others do the same. **C. S. LEWIS,** *Mere Christianity*

Do not store up for yourselves treasures on earth, where moth and rust destroy, and where thieves break in and steal. But store up for yourselves treasures in heaven, where neither moth nor rust destroys, and where thieves do not break in or steal; for where your treasure is, there your heart will be also. **MATTHEW 6:19-21, NASB**

But in your hearts set apart Christ as Lord. Always be prepared to give an answer to everyone who asks you to give the reason for the hope that you have. But do this with gentleness and respect.
1 PETER 3:15, NIV

Praise be to the God and Father of our Lord Jesus Christ! In his great mercy he has given us new birth into a living hope through the resurrection of Jesus Christ from the dead. **1 PETER 1:3, NIV**

"There was a real railway accident," said Aslan softly. "Your father and mother and all of you are—as you used to call it in the Shadow-Lands—dead. The term is over: the holidays have begun. The dream is ended: this is morning." . . . For them it was only the beginning of the real story. All their life in this world and all their adventures in Narnia had only been the cover and the title page: now at last they were beginning Chapter One of the Great Story, which no one on earth has read: which goes on for ever: in which every chapter is better than the one before. **C. S. LEWIS,** *The Last Battle*

An Exquisite Recipe

MRS. STOVER'S EXQUISITE FUDGE

4 cups sugar
1 large (12 oz.) can evaporated milk
1 stick butter

Cook in a heavy pan slowly, stirring often, as it sticks easily. Boil (325 degrees, if you have a candy thermometer) until the mixture forms a definite soft ball in cold water.

1 large (12 oz.) package semi-sweet chocolate chips
1 8 oz. jar marshmallow crème
1 teaspoon vanilla
dash of salt
1 cup chopped pecans or walnuts (optional)

Remove from heat and stir in chocolate chips, marshmallow crème, vanilla, salt, and nuts. Do not overbeat—only until well mixed and chips are melted. Pour into buttered 13x12-inch platter and cut into squares when cool. Makes about four pounds.

And since we're talking about hope and heaven, and both always offer MORE than you ever expected . . . here's one more recipe!

(Note: After these you'll need a bigger pair of pants. But why not live a little, ladies?)

ITALIAN CAKE
(The batter is beyond delicious!)

    1 stick butter
    1 ½ cup Crisco
    2 cups sugar
    5 egg yolks
    2 cups self rising flour
    1 teaspoon baking soda
    1 cup buttermilk
    1 teaspoon vanilla
    1 small can coconut
    1 cup chopped nuts
    5 egg whites, stiffly beaten

Cream butter and Crisco; add sugar. Beat until smooth. Add egg yolks and beat well. Combine flour and soda alternately with buttermilk. Stir in vanilla. Add coconut and nuts. Fold in egg whites.

Pour into 3 pans (9-inch size) that have been greased and floured. Bake 25 minutes at 350 degrees. Ice cake with Italian Cream Cheese Icing.

ITALIAN CREAM CHEESE ICING

    1 (8 oz.) package cream cheese, softened
    ½ stick butter
    1 box powdered sugar
    1 teaspoon vanilla
    Chopped nuts

Beat cream cheese and butter until smooth. Add sugar and mix well. Add vanilla. Beat until smooth. Spread on layers. Sprinkle top and sides with nuts.

About the Author

Call her a 21st-century Erma Bombeck with a pleasantly skewed twist! Julie Ann Barnhill's outrageous humor will indeed have you "laughing so hard you snort" and clapping your hands with glee. With her disarming wit and generous doses of vulnerability and authenticity, both on stage and in print, she's become a best-selling author and popular national speaker.

Julie's first featured book, *She's Gonna Blow! Real Help for Moms Dealing with Anger,* caught the attention of American television and radio producers nationwide, as did *'Til Debt Do Us Part: Real Help for Couples Dealing with Finances* in Canada and Britain. *Scandalous Grace* has garnered zillions of e-mails. Julie has appeared on such programs as *Oprah, CNN Sunday Morning,* Dick Clark's *The Other Half,* CNBC's *PowerLunch,* and the Canadian television show *It's a New Day.* Her radio spots include *National Public Radio, Janet Parshall's America*, the *Midday Connection* in Chicago, and a two-day interview that aired March 17–18, 2003, with radio legend Dr. James Dobson on *Focus on the Family.* Julie is also a contributing editor for *Today's Christian Woman.*

Julie is a spunky, sassy, and thought-provoking speaker. She challenges her audiences to "fasten their seat belts!" as she dispenses the lone antidote for remaining sane amidst life's roller-coaster ride of emotional, financial, physical, and spiritual ups and downs—the medicinal cure of guffaw-inducing, jaw-aching, "my stomach muscles hurt so much" laughter!

She is also the mother of three sometimes annoying, always amusing, challenging, stubborn, funny, and argumentative children. And wife to one hubby who has co-owned her dream of speaking and writing since 1984, the year they met. Amazingly, this man thinks she can do anything. *(Okay, anything but mend clothes. Her motto is: If you lose a button, buy a new shirt. Got a hole in your sock? Go buy a 12-pack.)*

Julie, her husband, and their three dependents live in a small (population 486, including decorative yard dwarfs) village located in western Illinois. In that town people use riding lawn mowers as all-terrain vehicles. In fact, Julie about jumped out of her new-neighbor skin when John Deere and Snapper tractors sputtered to the post-office door! It's a place where entertainment is somewhat limited to pulling up a lawn chair and watching a neighbor trim his 25-foot elm tree with a handsaw and rickety ladder. But it's also the kind of old-fashioned place where your neighbor makes you homemade meatballs in the middle of winter and brings them over "just because."

You can visit Julie Barnhill's Web site at: *www.juliebarnhill.com.*

If you are interested in having Julie Ann Barnhill speak at your special event, please contact her directly at her Web site or at *julie@juliebarnhill.com.*

Endnotes

CHAPTER ONE: I Know a Place

1. Mark 5:35-42, Eugene Peterson, *The Message* (Colorado Springs: NavPress, 2002), 1818–1819.
2. Mark 10:14, ibid., 1829.
3. Acts 17:28, *Holy Bible,* New International Version (Grand Rapids, Mich.: Zondervan, 1984).
4. 1 Corinthians 13:13, *The Message,* 2086.
5. Jeremiah 29:11, ibid., 1413.
6. John 14:1-3, *New American Standard Bible* (LaHabra, Calif.: The Lockman Foundation, 1977).

CHAPTER TWO: I Love a Mystery

1. A. W. Tozer, *Roots of Righteousness,* (Christian Publications, June 1986), as cited online at: http://www.abideinchrist.com/messages/col1v27.html, accessed January 2005.
2. 1 Peter 2:9, NASB.
3. Exodus 3:14, *The Message*, 109.
4. Exodus 3:6, ibid., 109.
5. Genesis 1:1, ibid., 20–22.
6. 2 Peter 3:8, ibid., 2220.
7. John 14:14, NASB.
8. John 3:16, ibid.
9. Colossians 1:26-27, *The Message,* 2145-2146.
10. Colossians 1:27, NASB.

11. 1 Peter 1:10-12, ibid.
12. Psalm 103:12, ibid.
13. Ephesians 1:9-11, *The Message,* 2126.
14. Ephesians 1:11-12, ibid.
15. Colossians 1:18-20, ibid., 2144.
16. Romans 11:33, NASB.
17. Ephesians 1:3, ibid.
18. Ephesians 1:17, ibid.
19. Ephesians 3:17, ibid.
20. Hebrews 6:17-19, ibid.
21. Revelation 1:8, ibid.
22. Hebrews 9:27, ibid.
23. Annie Dillard, *Teaching a Stone to Talk* (San Francisco: HarperPerennial, 1999), 40–41.
24. Ephesians 1:12, NASB.
25. Revelation 19:11, ibid.
26. As cited online at http://bibletools.org/index.cfm/fuseaction/ Def.show/RTD/ISBE/ID/6 681, accessed October 2004.
27. Matthew 13:11, NASB.
28. Luke 8:11-15, *The Message*, 1869–1870.
29. John 16:13-15, NASB.

CHAPTER THREE: Sweet Dreams Are Made of This
1. Romans 15:5, ibid.
2. In a portion of an essay titled, "The Few and the Many: Good Readers and Bad," Leland Ryken, ed., *The Christian Imagination* (Colorado Springs: WaterBrook Publishers, 2002), 225.
3. Jeremiah 29:10-11, *The Message,* 1413.
4. Jeremiah 29:12-14, ibid., 1414.
5. Jeremiah 1:4-5, ibid., 1343.
6. Anne Lamott, *Bird by Bird* (New York: Anchor, 1995), Introduction, xxiii.

CHAPTER FOUR: How Are You...Really?
1. As cited online at http://www.augnet.org/AugustineSECTION3/ AugustinesTimes/AugustineSpirituality/2196-Restlessness.htm, accessed November 2004.

2. C. S. Lewis, *Mere Christianity* (New York: Macmillian Publishing Co., 1943, 1945, 1952), 106.
3. Psalm 42:5, NASB.
4. C. S. Lewis, *Mere Christianity,* 106.
5. Colossians 3:17, NASB.
6. 1 John 2:15-17, *The Message,* 2224.

CHAPTER FIVE: It's the Small Things
1. Colossians 1:16-17, NASB.
2. Karen Dossel and her husband attended Eastview Community Church in Bloomington, Illinois, in which Hearts at Home first started.
3. Ecclesiastes 3:14, NASB.
4. John 11, ibid.
5. Matthew 26:17-29, ibid.
6. "My Hope Is Built" words: Edward Mote, 1836; music: William B. Bradbury, 1863.
7. Genesis 1:3, NASB.
8. Matthew 14:15-21, ibid.
9. Matthew 17:20, ibid.

CHAPTER SIX: This I Know to Be True
1. George Constanza, *Seinfeld,* Episode: The Dinner Party.
2. Lewis B. Smedes, *Keeping Hope Alive* (Nashville: Thomas Nelson, 1998), 8.
3. William Gurnall, *The Christian in Complete Armour,* as cited online at http://www.ccel.org/g/gurnall/armour/home.htm, accessed October 2004.
4. Jeremiah 29:10-11, *The Message,* 1413.
5. Isaiah 40: 27-31, ibid.,1284.
6. Jeremiah 31:3, ibid., 1418.
7. Jeremiah 29:11.
8. "My Hope Is Built."
9. Hebrews 11:4-6, NASB.
10. 1 Corinthians 13:13, ibid.

CHAPTER SEVEN: Are We There Yet?
1. *The Message,* 987.

2. Mark 1:15, NASB.
3. Romans 5:1-5, NIV.
4. *The Message,* 2039.
5. Jeremiah 29:13, NASB
6. NASB.
7. Ibid.

CHAPTER EIGHT: Going Up!

1. Revelation 1:7, NASB.
2. 1 Thessalonians 4:15-18, *The Message,* 2155-2156.
3. Titus 2:13, NASB.
4. 1 Thessalonians 4:13, 16, NASB.
5. John 14:1-3, *The Message,* 1949.
6. John 14:25-31, ibid., 1951.
7. 1 Corinthians 15:51-57, Ibid., 2092.
8. As cited online at http://www.khouse.org/articles/prophetic/20021201-444.html, accessed December 2004.
9. Matthew 24:32-44, *The Message,* 1794–1795.
10. Matthew 24: 6-8, ibid., 1793.
11. Psalm 23:4, NASB.

CHAPTER NINE: I'll Take You There

1. Hebrews 12:1-3, 12-13, *The Message,* 2196–2197.
2. NASB.
3. Revelation 21: 1-7, *The Message,* 2263.
4. Genesis 3:8, NASB.
5. Revelation 22:1-5, *The Message,* 2264.
6. "Holy, Holy, Holy" words: Reginald Heber, 1826, music: "Nicaea," John B. Dykes, in Hymns Ancient and Modern, 1861.
7. This portion is taken from the *Westminister Confession of Faith* written in 1646.

CHAPTER TEN: Until We Meet Again

1. Jude 1:24-25, *The Message,* 2235.

You found the something more
you were longing for
in *Exquisite Hope*.
Now it's time to experience
the incredible transformation that only
Scandalous Grace and *Radical Forgiveness* can provide!

"Witty, acerbic, and genuinely entertaining!"

SCANDALOUS GRACE – Julie Ann Barnhill

Scandalous Grace is the zing of encouragement every woman needs to transform her thoughts about herself and change her relationships, for the good. With gutsy honesty and stories that'll have you "laughing so hard you snort," Julie Barnhill reveals how you can live, day by day, in the knowledge of God's unconditional love in the midst of "loose ends." *ISBN 0-8423-8297-6*

RADICAL FORGIVENESS – Julie Ann Barnhill

What does it mean to *really* forgive those who have hurt you? To forgive yourself for the dumb things you've done? To forgive God for what he has—or hasn't—done? In this heartfelt, laugh-out-loud follow-up to *Scandalous Grace*, Julie Ann Barnhill shares the life-changing power of Jesus' sacrifice on the cross and helps readers transform their thoughts and relationships for good! *ISBN 1-4143-0031-X*

Available now at a bookstore near you!

Real Life. Honest Women. True Stories.

"This book will be like a breath of fresh air to your soul."
—SHEILA WALSH

Holding Out for a Hero: A New Spin on Hebrews – Lisa Harper

Every woman needs a hero. Now you can join Lisa Harper as she hits the road in search of the greatest hero of all time! You'll love this fresh new look at one of the New Testament's most inspiring books. And because traveling is always more fun with friends, you'll find a special DVD inside so you can sit in on Lisa's book group as they laugh, cry, and talk about the impact that the Hero of the ages is having on their lives today!
ISBN 1-4143-0276-2

"This book will change the way you think about the issue of submission."
—STEVE BROWN

The Myth of the Submissive Christian Woman – Brenda Waggoner

Scripture calls us to die to self—self-absorption, self-centeredness, self-righteousness, and self-indulgence—but nowhere does Scripture tell us to abandon all of the wonderful God-given gifts and talents that make us who we are. In *The Myth of the Submissive Christian Woman*, Brenda Waggoner dispels the myth that biblical submission requires women to become passive in their relationships with God and others and helps women live truthfully by putting God first in their lives and living according to his will.
ISBN 0-8423-7114-1

"Bask in the gentle wisdom of a trusted friend."
—RUTH MCGINNIS

Fairy Tale Faith – Brenda Waggoner

Drawing on such beloved fairy tales as *The Princess Bride*, *The Lion King*, and *Sleeping Beauty*, Christian counselor Brenda Waggoner explores the miracle that is God's grace. Tackling issues such as self-esteem, body image, and the difference between Christ-like submission and being nonassertive and weak-willed, Waggoner helps women live gracefully in the meantime while waiting for *happily ever after*.
ISBN 0 8423 7113 3

"This is the kind of woman I want to learn from!"
—KAY ARTHUR

The Hungry Heart – Lynda Hunter Bjorklund

Everyone longs for intimacy. As Christians we know that intimacy, significance, and acceptance can be found in the arms of a loving and gracious God. Dr. Lynda Hunter Bjorklund teaches women how to get to that place with God and find the deep relationship that comes from really knowing the One who created you.
ISBN 0-8423-7938-X

"Today's Christian woman should be proud to be termed a 'SHE.'"
—PUBLISHER'S WEEKLY

SHE – Rebecca St. James and Lynda Hunter Bjorklund

Today's media bombards women with messages that say, "You must be beautiful, thin, sexy, successful, strong, outgoing, and independent." But who does God say a woman should be? Get up close and personal with Rebecca St. James and Lynda Hunter Bjorklund as they expose the lies that drive women to distraction. And as they share their own struggles, heartaches, and successes, they reveal the truth of God's plan for women's lives.
ISBN 1-4143-0026-3

Available now at a bookstore near you!